Dad's Guide - How

INVEST IN STOCKS, SHARES, AND FUNDS

>>> A BEGINNER'S GUIDE TO GETTING STARTED <<<

PATRICK CARTER

Dad's Guide. How to Invest in Stocks, Shares, and Funds.
A beginner's guide to getting started.

Paperback ISBN: 9781998998708
eBook ISBN: 9781998998715

Contact: ppcarter73@outlook.com

Image credits: Front cover image: backup_studio – stock.adobe.com; Part one and part two images: Zdenek Sasek – stock.adobe.com; Part three image: Patrick Carter; Design, layout and typesetting: Patrick Carter.

Praise for Dad's Guide ...

"Superb, easy to read guide - even your wife can understand it!"

Melanie - the wise wife

About the author

I started investing in shares a few years after finishing University, on reflection knowing very little – some share trading went well, but my share investing was poor, and those mistakes cost money. That put me off investing in shares for another two decades!

A lot older, and a little wiser, I got back into investing in my mid-40's. One morning my 15-year-old son mentioned that he'd like to invest in shares when he got older and that I'd have to show him some time. That passing remark triggered a thought that grew into this book.

As I thought about this first Dad's Guide, I reflected on how little I had known in my younger years – and how much better I could have utilized my cash and savings through my 20's, 30's and 40's!

While I've been successful with study and work, it never came easy – I always felt that I had to work harder. I struggled with my GCSE's and did not enjoy school – but I was hungry to achieve, and academic qualifications can open doors, so I went on to study A-levels in Economics, Sociology and Business Studies, followed by a BSc in Managerial and Administrative Studies at Aston University in Birmingham. I fell into Chartered Accountancy, gaining experience in Audit, Corporate Tax, and Business Recovery, before moving into Corporate Finance, where I studied and passed a Diploma in Corporate Finance.

On the birth of our first child, 15 years ago, I quit my job to go freelance - working on interim projects. Over the years, having worked in Rationalization and Restructure, I moved into Change and Transformation and finally into the role of Group Finance Transformation Director in a couple of businesses, basically acting as an interpreter between Finance and IT departments to drive meaningful, effective change.

Research, study, and new experiences have shaped my life. I've now started the next chapter in my life, deciding to retire from employment, moving into full-time investing, property renovation, and writing a series of books ...

This Dad's Guide is written with humor, but I've tried to avoid the Dad jokes – as I don't want to embarrass my kids!

Best wishes,

Patrick Carter

CONTENTS

Introduction

If you want to become an intelligent investor, get started with this Dad's Guide, written in plain English with real-life examples. This easy-to-read guide covers how to get started, from selecting and using a dealing platform to shortlisting companies and determining target prices to buy and sell.

I share my trading experiences, including my ground rules for investing, demonstrating how to achieve substantial returns from trading, maximizing tax-free returns, and how to shortlist from thousands of funds.

Don't be crazy, be intelligent!

The world is a crazy place, and people do crazy things – technology has created a new generation of investors, quick off social media and onto their trading app making investments – often with little, or no, regard to business fundamentals.

Headlines captured this new age with the US activist investors creating a buying frenzy that sent the GameStop share price up from $20 to over $300 per share.

All this takes me back to my 20's and how a lack of knowledge and understanding cost me money – investing in the wrong stocks, and probably at the wrong time!

Companies are in business to make money, make a profit, and grow – that is what fundamentally values a business. In the US, stock market analysts believed GameStop was worth less than $20 per share, so they were 'shorting' the stock, effectively betting that the share price would fall. The activist investors managed to drive up demand for the shares, forcing the share price up – being the simple economics of supply and demand. Unfortunately, it was only ever going to be temporary, and many of those investors are either going to sell at a loss or be left holding shares worth a fraction of what they paid.

Another crazy thing is cryptocurrency, as is CFD trading (Contracts For Difference), as is foreign exchange trading, as is trading indexes.

Crazy is doing things you don't understand. It's like jumping on a motorbike and thinking it's simply a bike with a motor – wrong, a lot can go wrong, and a crash is inevitable!

So against this backdrop of crazy, my guidance is to ignore all that social media noise – be an intelligent investor, play it smart. Outperform your peers, not as a follower, but through applying knowledge and systematic, planned, risk-aware investing - slow but sure – and you'll be the one with the biggest smile!

Keep It Simple

It's incredible what you get taught. After seven years in High School studying for GCSE and A-Levels, I remember being told to KISS ... and thinking that should have been mentioned a lot, lot sooner!

I was taught with a double S because that second S stands for 'Stupid', which summed me up pretty well! But we don't need insults, so let's stick to KIS – Keep It Simple. That one little message applies to all parts of life – and it works well for investing in stocks, shares, and funds – so this book is about Keeping It Simple. It's always hard to simplify things, but that's what I've tried to do – to make this book easy to read, easy to follow, and easy to understand.

Embrace the concept of Keeping It Simple, make it the foundation on which you invest – I'll share how I keep my investing simple, using examples and sharing the Who, What, Why, When, and How I make money investing.

Navigating this book

Before launching into who I use to trade, how I select shares to trade, targeting prices at which to trade, or how to shortlist funds for investment, I thought it appropriate to create some context and develop a foundation of knowledge and understanding.

I believe time and effort are essential ingredients to successful investing – so please invest your time in this book, and then invest your time in research, monitoring, and planning your investments – this is not a 'get rich quick' story, but with your time and effort, the rewards can be very attractive!

Part 1 is all about 'Building the Foundations' – nothing too complicated, just a plain English background on stocks, stock markets, and interpreting the news and financial jargon – providing the foundations of knowledge needed to invest confidently with intelligence. Part 1 finishes with a chapter on getting started tax-efficiently in the UK.

Part 2 is focused on 'Investing and Trading in Shares' – covering each step with real-life examples and explanations, from proven techniques to trade in shares successfully to investing in shares for dividends, growth, and shareholder perks! Part 2 finishes with a chapter on spreadsheets, with examples and explanations of how I use them for my investing activities.

Part 3 is 'Investing in Funds'. Simplifying and using real-life examples to demystify this straightforward approach to investing. I work through how to shortlist from thousands of available funds, sharing the funds I shortlisted for my family and their recent performance.

Always remember, the value of investments could fall as well as rise, and you could get back less than you invest. So if you suffer from impatience, fear, greed, boredom, or addiction ... investing in shares and funds is probably not for you!

PART ONE:
Building the Foundations

On reflection:

"Investing in shares and the stock market is like having a teenage daughter – one day it can be loving towards you, other days silent, moody, or plain rude!"

CHAPTER 1

Company Ownership and Stock Markets

This chapter starts to build up the background on shares and share ownership and cover where shares are traded.

Sole Traders and Limited Companies

It all starts with a business ... if you set up your own business as a sole trader, you work for yourself and take all the risks and rewards personally. All your income, costs, and profits are then taxed through your Self Assessment tax return.

To reduce that personal liability, many people will set up their business as a limited company which creates a separate legal person. The ownership of the company is set up using shares. In a simple husband and wife business, this may be two ordinary shares with a nominal value of £1 each, the husband and wife each owning one share – so they are each 50% shareholders.

The shares in a business are called equity. Overdrafts and bank loans are called debt. Companies can raise finance from both debt and equity – so borrowing money from a lender, or selling shares to investors, employees, family, and friends, etc.

The limited company generates income from sales, incurs costs, and the difference is the profit – on which the business pays corporation tax. The remaining 'profit after tax' can either be retained in the business or paid out to the shareholders as a dividend.

Shares in limited companies are not traded; there is no marketplace for the shares. If a shareholder wishes to sell their shares, they will appoint advisers to value the business and their shares. This value may be challenging to achieve, as there may be few willing buyers for that equity.

Public Limited Company

As a business grows, the Limited company may seek to list on a Stock Market, becoming a public limited company (PLC). The listing makes the shares marketable, so buying and selling the shares becomes a lot easier. This is often done to raise new equity finance, to fund growth and expansion, but it is also done as an exit for the current investors, perhaps the founder or private equity backers.

That initial 'listing' on the Stock Market is called the Initial Public Offering (IPO).

London Stock Exchange

In the UK, our stock market is the London Stock Exchange. The London Stock Exchange is one of the oldest, dating back to 17th century London. In the old days, when I was a kid, it used to be a trading floor where members could buy and sell shares. Technology has caught up, and share trading is now almost entirely done electronically using state-of-the-art systems that can process over a million trades per day!

Companies on the London Stock Exchange range in size. There is the Main Market, with stricter compliance and governance requirements, and there is AIM – the Alternative Investment Market. AIM was launched in 1995 and requires less compliance and governance, being attractive to growth companies looking to access equity finance to fund further expansion.

Main Market

The performance of the Main Market is measured by several indexes which track company performance – the main stock index is called the Financial Times Stock Exchange 100, or the FTSE 100, also referred to as the Footsie.

A company's value is expressed as its Market Capitalisation (often shortened to Market Cap), being the number of shares in issue multiplied by the price per share. The FTSE 100 index comprises the largest listed companies by value, the FTSE 250 index comprises the next largest 250 companies (often called the Mid Cap), with the Small Cap Index comprising those outside the top 350.

The marketplace for goods and services is increasingly global, so the country a company is listed in doesn't necessarily reflect where it does most of its business. The London Stock Exchange is not a market for purely UK businesses. It includes UK businesses with operations worldwide, and it includes companies established in other countries, who have listed on the London Stock Exchange in recognition of it being a globally renowned stock exchange.

Index versus Company

The UK FTSE 100 is heavily weighted with Banking, Mining, and Pharmaceutical stocks – this means that they make up a large proportion of the overall index. If these sectors are impacted by local, national, or global events, the share price of the companies in these market sectors may decline, bringing the FTSE 100 index down. In the meantime, the share prices of other companies in other sectors of the FTSE 100, such as Media, Technology, or Consumer Goods, may well have risen in value.

So, while I like to be aware of what the FTSE 100 index is doing, I'm generally more interested in the actual share prices of the companies I'm invested in or following.

Companies can move between AIM and the Main Market, and they can move between the Main Market indexes - so, for example, from the FTSE 250 into the FTSE 100. Companies can also decide to leave the stock market, which is called delisting.

Stock Exchange Website

You can find shares prices, company information, and lists of which companies are in each index or market on the Stock Exchange website: www.londonstockexchange.com

If you click on the 'News and Prices' tab, you can build a filter to get the selection you want. I selected MAIN for Market, EQUITY for Investment Type, and FTSE 100 for Index. Those criteria returned 101 results, making me laugh, as I always thought the FTSE 100 was the biggest 100 companies listed in London. It turns out that the London Stock Exchange have some discretion on who is in or out of the index, so it's 'roughly' 100 ;-}

When you look at that company list, each company has a Stock Code, so for example, Anglo American is AAL, AstraZeneca is AZN, and Barclays Bank is BARC. This code is an important identifier.

Stock Exchanges worldwide

You will frequently see and hear about other stock exchanges worldwide, as what happens in one country often spills over into other countries and indexes. The main share indexes you'll hear about in other countries are:

- Germany – DAX index
- France – CAC index
- Hong Kong – Hang Seng index

- Japan – Nikkei index
- China – Shanghai index
- India - Sensex index, and Nifty index

The USA has several indexes frequently in the news. These are primarily:

- S&P 500 index
- Dow Jones Industrial Average index
- NASDAQ Composite index

REMEMBER – an index is simply a collection of companies. It could be by size or by sector or country.

Stocks / Shares

These terms are frequently used interchangeably, each meaning the same thing. In the UK, we frequently use shares in reference to a single company, while stocks refer to more than one company, for example, 'the stock market'.

Nominal Value

If you look at Barclays Bank shares, you'll see BARC Ord 25p, which means they are Ordinary Shares of 25p nominal value. This has little to do with the current share price, but it helps you identify what you are buying.

By using the London Stock Exchange website, I can filter and search the listed companies, see what the company code is, the share type, nominal value, and likely share price range – so when I go to buy the shares, I'm confident that I'm buying the right shares.

Share ownership

If you invest in a listed company, you become a shareholder – a part-owner of that business. As such, you can benefit from the growth in its share price from its success, receive the dividends it pays out, and some companies also offer perks or rewards for being a shareholder.

Suppose you invest £1,500 buying 1,000 shares at 150 pence each, plus dealing fees and stamp duty. Many companies pay an interim dividend and a final dividend, typically six months apart. Say you were paid an interim dividend of 2 pence per share and a final dividend of 4 pence per share, your total dividends during the year would be 6 pence per share, worth £60. During the same period, the share price could have increased from

150 pence to 170 pence, which if you sold the shares would generate a capital gain of 20 pence per share, being £200.

Dividends and Capital Gains are taxed differently, which we cover in Part 2 ... as you can make both of these tax-free!

Opening and Closing prices

Trading hours are between 8.00 am and 4.30 pm, Monday to Friday. Excluding Bank Holidays.

If you monitor share prices, you will spot that the last price you see at the end of one day is not necessarily the next day's opening price.

The opening price results from the opening auction that takes place before the market opens, from 7.50 am to 8 am. This is when news, tips, global events, etc., get priced into the opening share prices.

The last closing price is from the previous days closing auction, which takes place immediately after the market closes, from 4.30 pm to 4.35 pm.

The direction of opening and closing prices might suggest the market sentiment for the day. If you saw the share's price finish the day at one price but then open the following day several pence cheaper, you might expect to have a morning of decline – but share prices bounce around, they are the result of buyers, sellers, and news around the world – you can be watching the share price decline at one point of the day, then check again and it's rebounded or rallied.

Broker coverage

Listed companies will have brokers and analysts from the big institutions publish reports on them. This includes assessing the business trading, profits, cashflows, debt, etc. – historical and prospective, and views on management, acquisitions, disposals, new products/services, entry into new markets, etc. These reports often conclude with a BUY, SELL, or HOLD recommendation.

Some of the big-name brokers/analysts include Barclays, HSBC, Bank of America, Credit Suisse, JP Morgan, UBS, Morgan Stanley, Peel Hunt, Citi, and many more.

These broker/analyst reports can be an interesting read, and when published, can have an impact on the share price by impacting the demand to buy or sell those shares.

Bear Market

The Bear Market is a miserable place. It's a marketplace of declining share prices, encouraging the selling of shares. It is associated with widespread pessimism and negative sentiments.

Bull Market

We love the Bull Market, particularly if we are holding shares! It's a marketplace where share prices are rising or are expected to rise. It is associated with happiness, optimism, and investor confidence.

!! WARNING !!

As a shareholder, you also face the risk that the business may not perform well. The value of your shares could go down in value, the company may pay no dividends, and the worse case, it could collapse – going bust and leaving you with no or very little value.

For example, in April 2019, Debenhams Plc entered administration and delisted from the London Stock Exchange. Anyone left holding shares would have faced a 100% loss. Luckily, if you followed the news and watched the warning signs, you could have either avoided buying the shares or exited your shareholding with some value before the collapse.

Having been burnt and lost money on AIM shares decades ago, I now reduce my risk and stick to the Main Market and companies in the FTSE100 and FTSE250 - but even big companies can fail!

CHAPTER 2

The Economics of Share Prices

I apologize in advance - this chapter gets a bit academic, building up your knowledge ... but I think it's necessary.

This chapter seeks to share some of the factors that influence a share price, as being aware of these can help you decide whether to buy or sell an investment. We also summarise some of the technical terms that you'll frequently see. Let's begin with a bit of financial economics:

Efficient Market Hypothesis

At some stage during my studies, a long, long time ago, we covered the topic of the Efficient Market Hypothesis. The hypothesis sets out that all available information is already priced into the share price of companies in an efficient market. The implication is that it is impossible to "beat the market" consistently as the prices should only react to new information.

I think this hypothesis is intriguing. When you read that article in the news-paper, magazine, Blog post, Bulletin Board, etc., that information is already priced into the share price. If you invest, are you expecting the share price to leap when everyone else has read that article? ... the news that is publicly available and already priced into the share price ... see what I mean, an interesting argument!

Value of a Company

In Corporate Finance, there are several ways of valuing a business. You can look at comparable companies and use what's called a multiple of earnings approach, you could look at the net assets and value it based on what you can realize from selling those assets, and you can use something referred to as Discounted Cash Flows (DCF).

DCF is a valuation method based on several assumptions and limitations, which forecasts the cash flows generated by a business out into future years. As the concept recognizes the time value of money, being a pound received next year is worth less than a pound received today, it discounts the value of future cash flows. The result of adding up these discounted future cash flows is the Net Present Value – so the valuation today.

Importantly, events that reduce the future cash flows will reduce the company valuation, and events that increase the future cash flows will increase the company valuation. Something that affects the short term will have a higher impact. Something that happens way out in the medium to long term may have a lesser impact, as it will be discounted for the time value of money ...

Supply and Demand

A fundamental concept in economics is supply and demand and how supply and demand determine the price in a competitive market.

If we think of share prices using the concept of supply and demand, we know that a listed company has a number of shares issued, so that is the available 'supply' being traded on the stock exchange. Trading is the buying and selling of those shares based on the demand for those shares. So if lots of people want to buy the shares, this increases demand and is likely to push the price upwards, as existing shareholders may have no interest in selling the shares until they see a share price that motivates them to sell.

Imagine another potential global pandemic – investors may worry about another stock market crash, so they would sell their shares to be holding cash or other safer assets. When demand for buying the shares falls and the supply of shares being sold increases, supply and demand force the share price down.

You could also think of the same scare impacting the short-term cashflows of the business, which according to our DCF valuation, would mean the value of the company will be reduced as anything happening in the short term has a much greater impact.

These are concepts to help you better anticipate and understand share prices; they will not help you calculate the share price – that's even difficult for the experts!

Acquisitions

When a company is bought, it's called an acquisition or a takeover. The company making the acquisition will spend a lot of money on advisors and lengthy due diligence. This may include visits to the business locations, interviews with management, speaking to key customers and suppliers, and a 'data room' full of financial and non-financial information.

The point is, the acquiring company doesn't take ownership of the target by looking at a bulletin board or share price graph. They put the time and investment into doing it correctly. As small investors, we don't get access to management and a data room of confidential information, but we should be thorough with our research before buying.

If a company becomes an acquisition target, its share price will increase as it is widely acknowledged that takeovers are done at a premium to the share price. That is unless it's in financial distress and sold for £1!

An acquisition may also increase the acquiring company's share price. The investment should bring new revenue and profits, new customers, products, markets, etc., and it's always believed that duplicate costs can be stripped out, being the synergy benefits.

The reality is that many acquisitions are over-priced, too much is paid, and the synergy savings are never fully recognized. The investment can also spread existing management and teams too thin, which may negatively affect the core business. That's why you'll sometimes see news about an acquisition, and the share price of the company announcing the acquisition goes down!

Disposals

Sometimes a big business can be worth more as a sum of its parts. Acquisitions bring complexity, often with different cultures, different computer systems, different risks, etc. It usually takes the appointment of a new Chief Executive to implement a strategic review and a transformation program, often driving out complexity, risk, low profit, or loss-making operations, products, or services.

Announcing the disposal of non-core businesses in overseas countries, different sectors, etc., to focus on core markets can improve the companies share price.

Share price

As a new investor, don't be fooled into thinking low share prices are better than higher share prices. In reality, the actual share price tells you nothing.

Let's look at Company A, and Company B:

Company A has 1 million shares in issue, with each share selling at 100p (i.e., £1.00).

Company B has 2 million shares in issue, with each share selling at 50p.

Both Company A and Company B have the same valuation, £1 million.

Assuming no dealing costs, etc., if you invested £1,000 in each company and made a 10% profit selling each, you would have the same gain. Let's break that down:

Company A - £1,000 buys 1,000 shares of £1.00p each. If you sold the shares and made a 10% return, selling at £1.10 and making 10p, the total return is 1,000 shares multiplied by 10p, which is £100.

Company B - £1,000 buys 2,000 shares of 50p each. If you sold the shares and made a 10% profit, selling them at 55p and making 5p, the total return is 2,000 shares multiplied by 5p, which is also £100.

Very simply, a 10% return on a £1,000 investment is going to be £100 regardless of the share price!

Earnings Per Share

The Earnings Per Share, abbreviated as EPS, is a financial measure of performance often quoted in financial statements and articles. The calculation is to take the company's earnings, being its net profit, and dividing that by the number of shares in issue. The higher the earnings per share, the more profitable the business is viewed to be.

This 'basic' EPS can be amended to become an 'Adjusted' EPS, where perhaps one-off profits have been excluded from the calculation. There is also a 'Diluted' EPS, which considers further potential issues of shares – for example, from the exercise of stock options, so the calculation reflects the higher number of shares.

Comparing EPS between companies and different sectors raises loads of questions. I'm left thinking, 'So What!?!', not all those earnings are paid out to shareholders anyway – some earnings are retained as cash in the business or are held for future growth. Some people may find it a helpful metric for selecting which shares to buy or sell, but I never have – it's not something I consider.

Price Earnings Ratio

The Price Earnings Ratio, PE ratio, or P/E ratio, is another financial measure that you see everywhere. The calculation takes the company's share price and divides it by the Earnings Per Share.

For example, if the share price was 100 pence per share, and the EPS was 10 pence, the PE ratio would be 10 times, typically expressed as 10x.

A high PE suggests the shares have good growth prospects, with increased earnings in the future ... but it might also indicate that the shares are expensive and over-priced! Likewise, a low PE might suggest low growth prospects, but it might also be a sign that the shares are cheap!

High PE ratios are often found in the Technology, Electronic, and Health-care sectors, in start-ups and high growth companies, and small-cap companies. Investors who favor high PE's are called Growth investors.

Low PE ratios are often found in the Utilities, Mining, and Tobacco sectors, which are often larger-cap companies. Investors who favor low PE's are called Value investors.

While many investors and analysts may find it a useful metric, I don't – it raises as many questions as it answers, so I don't use PE ratios for deciding what and when to buy or sell.

Profits

Unless you are a charity, most companies will be in business to make a profit – simply viewed as your income (revenue from sales) less your costs.

Company accounts seem to be getting more and more complex. We have accounting standards so complex that they need interpreting – whatever happened to Keeping It Simple, and simple is best!

We also refer to profit in many different ways, but often mean the same thing. Profits are called earnings, net profit, profit after tax, retained earnings, etc. – when you look at any numbers, just focus on the profit after tax line. Profit after tax is what a business has left to reinvest or payout to shareholders. Look at how it compares to the prior year, is it growing or declining? A falling profit is bad news!

Cash

Cash and cash flows are significant. Unlike profit, which companies can manipulate in so many ways through accounting treatments, cash and cash flow are a lot harder to manipulate – it's based on either cash in or cash out!

Over a year, you ideally want to see cash being generated – so more cash inflows than cash outflows. Cash outflows can be going on financing debt and repaying debt and capital investments in property, machinery, etc.

While a company might have cash balances, you're more likely to see it reported as a net debt position – so debt less cash. The higher the net debt, the more risk in the business. Many businesses that have gone bust in the past are due to the burden of large amounts of debt.

Dividend policy

Dividends are the return of cash to shareholders. This provides an income to investors, while they may hold the shares for future growth. Many different types of investors may seek out companies with good dividend payouts, from large pension funds to retired individuals, to me!

An attractive and reliable dividend policy can build trust and confidence in the business. Maintaining and delivering a dividend policy suggests a strong, stable, and well-managed, profitable business that supports the share price.

Dividend yield

The dividend yield is the return generated by a dividend. It is calculated as the dividend in pence, divided by the share price in pence.

For example, on 4th March 2021, I read a news article entitled:

"Aviva eyes cash handouts after a record year in savings and retirements."

The article noted a 14 pence per share dividend. The share price was showing 388.5p, so a quick calculation ... the dividends per share of 14 pence divided by the share price of 388.5 pence, equals 0.036 which when multiplied by 100 becomes 3.6% - quite an attractive dividend yield.

As the share price rises, the dividend yield will reduce – but that also means as the share price falls, the dividend yield increases – so an attractive dividend policy can attract investors. As we know from supply and demand theory, that demand should raise the share price.

Ex-Dividend

There are some key dates to know about companies' dividends. The ex-dividend, ex-div, or XD date represents the date on or after which you no longer qualify for the announced dividend. So if you purchase the shares before the ex-dividend date and hold onto them until after that ex-dividend date, you will receive the dividends.

The share price should theoretically decline by the value of the dividend on the ex-dividend date, as the company's net assets will decrease by the value of the dividend.

Using my example of the Aviva dividend, an internet search for the Aviva Plc investor page provided the Ex-Div date as 8th April. It confirmed a dividend of 14 pence per share, with a Payment Date of 14th May. It also provided the Record Date as 9th April.

The Record Date is when the company examines its list of shareholders to determine who is eligible for the dividend.

Share Buybacks

Companies will often use surplus cash to buyback their own shares, which are then canceled. It is effectively a dividend without shareholders receiving any cash, as the canceled shares should increase the share price.

Buybacks allow a company some flexibility, as paying out dividends becomes an expectation that negatively impacts the share price if it changes. By doing both dividends and share buybacks, a company can maintain a consistent dividend policy.

Value of Sterling

A weak pound is good for investors - as a weak pound against the dollar, or the euro, means that overseas earnings will be worth more. This will have a positive impact on the value of large foreign-earning multinationals.

For example, if the exchange rate is $1.40 : £1, then a $1,000 of earnings, when converted back into pounds, are worth £714. If the pound weakens, so it's now buying fewer dollars i.e., if the exchange rate drops to $1.30 : £1, then $1,000 of earnings will convert back into the higher sterling value of £769.

US Influence

It is said that when the US sneezes, the UK catches a cold - it means that whatever happens in the US markets ripples out to other markets. Given the time difference between the UK and the US, you will usually see a normal morning of trading in the UK, then all of a sudden lunch arrives, the US wakes up - and share prices can start to rally or decline.

Day Traders

This is a type of share trading where any purchases made in the day are sold the same day – whether it makes a profit or a loss. This approach is used to reduce risk, as the investments are likely to be in smaller or riskier companies - anything could happen overnight or over a weekend that could severely impact the share price. By converting back to cash at the end of the day, any losses have been stemmed before they can get any worse.

This is not an approach I adopt, but it is worth understanding that some people do this. Day traders are likely to more active as the market opens in the morning, buying into shares, and again nearer close of play, selling shares.

Chartist

This term describes someone who uses charts and graphs of past share prices to forecast the future share price trend. It is easy to dismiss this approach, as the charts may mean nothing to you, and you often see warnings that say, "Past performance is no guarantee of future results."

There are several types of analysis and phrases that you may come across. These include moving averages, candlesticks, support and resistance, and pullbacks.

Moving Averages

50-day and 200-day moving averages get quoted in analysis. A moving average is simply the closing share prices each day for the last 50 days or 200 days, added together then divided by either the 50 or the 200.

If the moving average is rising, that's a positive sign of growth in the share price. If the moving average is declining, that's a negative sign of a declining share price.

Candlesticks

I've seen – but never used - share price graphs that display candlesticks, which is a visual way to present multiple bits of data. When you look at a trading day, the share price opens at one level, then during the day it may go up and down, so the High and Low prices are noted, and at the end of the day you have the closing price.

If you imagine a graph with the share price values going up on the left and the days along the bottom, candlesticks are vertical lines for each trading day. The top of the candlestick is the high price, the bottom of the candle-stick is the low price, a horizontal dash cutting across the candlestick represents the opening price, and another represents the closing price. A thick body shows that range between the opening and closing prices, colored white or green if the price was going up, or colored black or red if the price was going down.

Support and Resistance

I use this technique a lot, and it works. If you look at the daily, weekly, and monthly share price graphs, you will typically see a pattern of up and downs. Support and resistance are the terms used to describe the pattern of repeated peaks and troughs. By following the share price graph, you will start to see the support and resistance levels.

As the share price drops, demand for the shares increases, and the price starts to increase – that low point becomes the support level or the floor. As the share price rises, profit-taking from selling may cap the increase, causing the share price to start declining. The high point is the resistance level or the ceiling.

By watching and determining the support and resistance levels, you can conclude your entry points and exit points for trading. We cover this with examples in Part 2.

Pullbacks

When there's been some upward momentum in the share price following an event or announcement, it may experience a pullback as investors take profits and sell their shares. Supply and demand's principles mean that the share price will decline due to the increased supply of shares. Still, the fundamental reason for the upward momentum remains, suggesting the share price will resume going up after this pullback. This is why pullbacks become a buying opportunity.

CHAPTER 3

Understanding the News

This chapter captures some of the things I've recently read online and in the papers that I think are worthy of discussion and explanation. Reading and understanding the news helps you identify what you might like to buy, sell, hold, or trade.

Trading updates & Financial Results

These updates often come with a comment that the "shares rallied" or "shares fell back" on the announcement. If the article was interesting, it's worth adding that business to your reading list – do some research on it and follow the share price charts for a few days to see whether that initial "rally", when the share price increased, has fallen back with investors profit-taking. Also, look for those previous support and resistance levels. If the share price fell, do you think the business is still fundamentally strong and will bounce back?

Profit Taking

When an article refers to profit-taking, it simply means that investors who bought at a lower price are selling at a higher price to make some profit.

As a share price increases beyond your purchase price, there's a natural desire to sell and 'take your profit'. Holding your nerve sometimes pays off, as the price might continue to increase, but it could also fall back and then continue to decline and never reach those previous highs!

Director Share Dealings

I don't let this influence me too much. Still, it's worth noting that the closest people to the performance and likely future of a company are those running it, such as the Chairman, Chief Executive, Finance Director, Managing Director, Operations Director, etc. When these directors sell their shares, it could be a sign of trouble ahead … when they buy shares, it could be a sign of their confidence in the future.

Director dealings must be notified to the London Stock Exchange within strict deadlines. It is publicly available information. The reason for the share dealing is less evident unless it is an award of shares for contractual performance, being part of their salary package, in which case the notification will set out how many shares were awarded under the scheme.

The number of shares bought or sold should be looked at compared to that person's holding. If they already hold 100,000 shares and buy another 10,000, that's only a small proportion, so that might mean very little. If they doubled their holding from 100,000 to 200,000 shares, that might be a significant signal. The same concept goes for sales. If they sold 10% of their holding, maybe no big deal … but if they sold everything, it helps to understand why!

The Stock Exchange has rules that prevent directors from dealing in shares during particular 'closed' times, these include during the preparation of the financial results, or if there is information that is not publicly known that could impact the share price, this could be an acquisition, disposal or some other significant event.

The 'signals' from director share dealing are widely known, so while a cluster of 3 or more directors selling shares might be a sign of trouble ahead, you must be mindful that a group of directors in a troubled company could also rally together and buy shares, to give the impression that all is good in the company.

Housing market data

You will see regular news on how the housing market is performing – average prices, sales, etc., or news that should help the housing market, such as stamp duty holidays, 95% mortgages, etc.

This market background can help form your view on the current trading conditions and prospects of the listed housebuilders, such as Taylor Wimpey plc, Persimmon Plc, and Barratt Developments plc, etc. – all in the FTSE 100 index, or the likes of Bellway plc, Redrow plc, Balfour Beatty plc, etc. in the FTSE 250 index. If you are researching house builders, consider looking on review sites such as TrustPilot, to see what the buyers of those properties are saying.

The housing market will also impact the suppliers of building materials, so the likes of Ibstock plc, Travis Perkins plc, Howden Joinery Group plc, etc. – all in the FTSE 250 index.

You can also think broader than house builders and building materials. What about estate agents? For example, Rightmove plc.

As the government will partially compensate lenders of 95% loan to value mortgages if homeowners fail to pay their mortgage, this boost to the housing market could also help out the banking sector... they'll lend more, increasing their income from fees and interest, with less risk!

Jobless data

US jobless data can have a ripple effect globally, impacting the US, Europe, and UK stock markets. Data is often monthly, so good news or bad news might reverse one month later.

Manufacturing data

It helps you understand how industrial firms may be performing. Are they busy? quiet? How does that impact the rest of the supply chain?

Inflation

Worries about rising inflation, in any country, typically knock back the share prices as it raises expectations of increases in interest rates, which create an additional cost in business, lowering profits.

Taxation

Anything suggesting higher taxes, either corporate taxation or individual taxation, is likely to dampen share prices. It reduces the after-tax profits of a business and could reduce personal spending and consumer demand.

Leverage

This is when you borrow money to buy more shares. It's high risk. If the shares you purchase fall in value, you may have to sell them for a loss to repay your loan.

The US fund, Archegos, hit the headlines in March 2021 as it was forced to sell a load of investments when it was caught out with too much debt after the shares it held fell in value. That sudden sale of shares impacted the supply and demand dynamics, reducing the share prices and sending a ripple of concern across world stock markets.

Days later, the news commented that the FTSE 100 was set to rally as worries over the implications of the Archegos Fund's blow-up began to dissipate on the global markets. This would have created buying opportunities for some investors.

Margin Call

This is when a lending broker may become worried about its exposure and demand that the investor pays down some of its debt. This is why the Archegos Fund blew up as it had to sell shares to honor the obligation.

FAANGs

While I might think of Dracula movies or getting my teeth stuck into something, this is an acronym that crops up frequently and refers to the stocks of five significant American technology companies – being Facebook, Amazon, Apple, Netflix, and Alphabet. Alphabet was previously known as Google, which explains the G!

IPO's

Initial Public Offering – when a company 'lists' its shares for trading on a stock exchange for the first time.

SPACs

This stands for Special Purpose Acquisition Company, formed to raise money through an Initial Public Offering (IPO) to buy another company. At the time of the IPO, SPACs have no existing business operations – it's purely an empty 'shell' company.

Investment Trust

This is a company typically set up by asset management firms. The company is listed on the stock exchange, with the funds raised from the share sale then used to invest in different assets, e.g., Technology stocks, Real Estate, etc.

REITs

This stands for Real Estate Investment Trust, a company that owns, operates, or finances real estate investments. This allows individual investors to earn dividends from real estate investments without getting involved in properties themselves.

ETF's

Exchange-Traded Funds are, as the description says, funds that are traded on the stock market just like shares in companies. The most popular ETF's are index trackers, which are cheaper and faster than buying up shares in each company. We cover funds in Part 3.

ETC's

Exchange-Traded Commodities – these are raw materials like gold, oil, or agricultural products. Investing in the ETC allows you to track the price of the underlying asset without having to take ownership of kilograms of gold or liters of oil … and the storage that entails!

Short Selling

This is a higher-risk strategy that involves selling borrowed shares in the belief that the price will drop. You then buy the shares at the lower price to repay the shares you sold at the higher price, making the difference as your profit. This used to be reserved for professional investors in hedge funds and large institutions. The spread of free/cheap trading platforms has extended this high-risk approach to individual investors.

Robinhood

Robinhood is a popular commission-free trading app in the US. It was frequently in the news during early 2021, with Robinhood traders following message boards on Reddit to drive up the price of GameStop.

Robinhood has faced criticism as the ease of free trading can downplay the risks and lead novices astray.

GameStop

This US-listed video game retailer was in the news a lot in early 2021. It had been trading around $20 per share, and big investors had shorted the stock, expecting it to fall and make them a profit. Activist investors gathered on Reddit message boards to go against the short-sellers and buy GameStop shares. The increased demand drove the share price up to over $340 per share!

The short sellers were forced to buy into the rising share price to mitigate some of their risk – which increased the demand and helped the share price rise further. The short sellers lost a lot of money.

If you look at business fundamentals, the GameStop valuation cannot be supported by traditional means. It became a 'meme' stock supported by a cult of activist investors – a completely new phenomenon.

Deliveroo

In March 2021, this food delivery start-up was the UK's biggest new IPO listing in a decade. Still, its share price plunged 30% after trading started – being a sign that investors are becoming wary of these so-called 'growth' stocks – being companies promising fast growth and future profits but that have yet to make a profit.

Some of the City's largest institutional investors, such as Aviva, Legal & General, and M&G, had ruled out investing in the business before it floated. Concerns included its working practices and the dual-class share structure, which gives founder Will Shu greater control.

Cryptocurrency / Cryptoassets

I don't understand or trust cryptocurrency and have avoided learning about it, as I never intend to invest in it! It appears too volatile to become a mainstream currency.

There are now thousands of varieties; Bitcoin, Ripple, Litecoin, and Ethereum have recently been in the news. You frequently hear about Bitcoin, with staggering growth in value and the likes of Elon Musk buying it and announcing Tesla will start accepting it as payment.

Crypto means hidden or secret, reflecting the secure technology that makes it anonymous. It is a type of electronic cash, but a central bank or government does not manage it. This creates significant risk, with no bank or central authority protecting you. If your funds disappear, no one is responsible for helping you get your money back.

With an increase in cryptocurrency scams in early 2021, the UK's Financial Conduct Authority (FCA) has warned that investors should be prepared to lose *"all their money"* if they choose to invest in cryptocurrency products offering high returns.

Overweight

This is what happens during a pandemic, you stop exercising, eat and drink more, and yep, you become overweight!

It is also an analyst's or broker's opinion that a stock will outperform over the next 12 months. Think of it as trying to beat an index-tracking fund; you would hold more of the stocks expected to outperform, being 'overweight' in those stocks in relation to the others in the index.

Underweight

Nope, not a problem for me, far from it!

From the analyst's or broker's opinion, you might want to sell these as they are expected to underperform.

CHAPTER 4

Being Alert to Fraud and Scams

There used to be a time when bogus, fraudulent scams were pretty obvious – poorly worded emails or letters full of typing errors. Those days have gone, but some of the techniques remain the same ... pressure to make a quick decision or miss out on the deal!

Social media, websites, and search engines make fake news and scams so much easier to legitimize. While scams often offer high returns to tempt you, that high return is generally a warning sign of a scam, so scammers may offer more realistic returns to make their offer appear more legitimate.

Scams are becoming increasingly sophisticated. Scams can be advertised in newspapers, magazines, and online as genuine investment opportunities. Fraudsters can be articulate and financially knowledgeable, with credible-looking websites, testimonials, and materials that are hard to distinguish from the real thing. It's relatively easy to publish a professional-looking website, create marketing material and even publish a book nowadays!

Always be wary if you receive an unexpected phone call, message, email, or letter, pressurizing you to invest quickly or promising returns that sound too good to be true – generally, the higher the return promised, the more likely it's a high-risk investment or scam.

My dodgy email example

I received an email with a timestamp of 01:47 from a 'Sum Bitcoin' with the title *'Your chance has arrived!'*. Mmm, yes, I'm sure that's going to be reliable!

The main body of the email included 'Read more' icons. Links are generally not an intelligent thing to click through. That's where the trouble starts - so I ignored those.

The hilarious proposal used cutting-edge technology terms that made me smile. It sounded like a tech word mash-up – would you believe this pitch:

"A user simply makes an initial deposit into the platform, usually of £200 or more, and the automated trading algorithm goes to work. Using a combination of data and machine learning, the algorithm knows the perfect time

to buy digital assets low and sell high, maximizing users profit."

So, this was looking even more like a scam! The last bit of the email went on to summarise a live experiment on the This Morning show:

"Holy deposited £200 live on the show. Within 3 minutes, she had success-fully increased her initial funds to £323.18p. That's a £123.18p profit"

It's pretty obvious that anyone with such a great get rich quick solution would ... simply get rich! Why try to get others to part with their money? Oh yeah, because it's a scam!

Financial Conduct Authority (FCA)

Scam firms offering or promoting products or investment opportunities are unlikely to be authorized or regulated by the FCA. You can check on the FCA website for firms to avoid.

If you deal with an unauthorized firm, you will not be covered by the Financial Ombudsman Service or Financial Compensation Scheme if things go wrong.

Spot the warning signs

- **Unexpected contact** - traditionally, scammers cold-call, but contact can also come from online sources, e.g., email or social media, post, word of mouth, or even in person at a seminar or exhibition.

- **Time pressure** – they might offer you a bonus or discount if you invest before a set date or say the opportunity is only available for a short period.

- **Social proof** – they may share fake reviews and claim other clients have invested or want in on the deal.

- **Unrealistic returns** – fraudsters often promise tempting returns that sound too good to be true, such as much better interest rates than elsewhere. However, scammers may also offer realistic returns to seem more legitimate.

- **False authority** - using convincing literature and websites, claiming to be regulated, speaking with authority on investment products.

- **Flattery** – building a friendship with you to lull you into a false sense of security.

- **Remote access** – scammers may pretend to help you and ask you to download software or an app so they can access your device. This could enable them to access your bank account or make payments using your card.

Source: www.fca.org.uk/scamsmart

Remember – anything promising get rich quick or high returns are likely to be either high-risk, worthless, overpriced, or even non-existent shares, bonds, or other investment opportunities.

Stay alert, Stay clear, Stay safe!

CHAPTER 5

Getting Started ... Tax Efficiently

This chapter sets out how to get set up with a trading account tax-efficiently in the UK.

Tax year

The tax year runs from 6th April to 5th April. We are in the 2021/22 tax year, which runs from 6th April 2021 to 5th April 2022.

Individual Savings Accounts (ISAs)

The UK Government launched ISAs back in 1999, replacing similar tax-efficient products. The great thing about ISAs is that you do not pay tax on any interest earned in a Cash ISA, and you do not pay tax on any income from dividends or capital gains from buying and selling shares in a Stocks and Shares ISA.

If you complete a Self Assessment tax return, you do not need to declare any ISA interest, dividends, or capital gains on it.

When ISA's were first launched, the initial annual allowance was set at £7,000 per tax year. Over the years, this has increased to £20,000 per tax year and has remained at that level for the last few years. The 2021/22 tax year allowance can be invested in one type of ISA account or split across some or all of the other ISA types. You are only allowed to pay £4,000 into the Lifetime ISA.

Your ISA account remains open when the tax year finishes, allowing you to continue earning tax-free income and gains on that ISA balance, and depending on the tax rules, allowing you to invest more money tax-free each year.

I transferred my Cash ISA balances to a Stocks and Shares ISA years ago, as I figured I could earn more from shares than I could on the low-interest rates. I'm 48 years old, so I'm not eligible for the Lifetime ISA, which is restricted to those aged between 18 and 40 years old.

The Lifetime ISA was launched to help get people on the property ladder for the first time or contribute to retirement savings. You can invest up to a maximum of £4,000 per year and receive a 25% government bonus. You can then use your remaining allowance to invest in a Cash or a Stocks and Shares ISA.

Tax rules for ISAs can change, and their benefits depend on your circumstances, but they appear to be a great way to get started investing in shares in the UK in 2021/22.

It would help if you considered how much you are likely to invest, then check out various providers' fees. Do a comparison between providers, calculating the different costs – platform fixed fees, platform variable fees, and trading costs.

General Investment Accounts

In addition to my stocks & shares ISA (which Barclays Bank calls an Investment ISA), I also have an investment account and investment saver account for additional investing. Any cash is held in the investment saver account, earning a little interest, and is immediately available for share trading through the linked investment account.

With the Barclays Smart Investor app, I can trade from either the ISA or the general investment account by simply selecting which one to use from the drop-down menu.

With the general investment account, you will need to track your interest, dividends, and capital gains and add these to your annual Self Assessment tax return.

Maximizing Tax-Free Opportunities

Ideally, you want to move £20,000 into your stocks & shares ISA every tax year to trade tax-free. Also, you want to trade using a general investment account to use your £12,300 capital gains tax allowance and £2,000 allowance for dividend income.

A married couple benefits from two ISA allowances, two CGT allowances, and two dividend allowances each tax year. That's a lot of tax-free potential!

Platforms / Providers

I've used several different banks over the years, between current accounts, savings accounts, share dealing accounts, and mortgage accounts. At some point, many years ago, I moved to Barclays Bank, and now virtually everything is with them – I've been pleasantly impressed and have felt thoroughly supported over the years (thanks Lee!), so that's my bank of choice.

I'm sure most banks will have a similar ISA and share dealing offering, so just check out your bank's website, check your online account or ask in their branch.

There also seems to be a constant supply of new trading account apps being launched by who knows who. Many seem to adopt the 'Freemium' model, where some functionality is provided for free while additional helpful functionality is a paid-for premium, while others are free or appear to be free!

A quick internet search for "share trading apps UK" delivers loads of names and articles. Frequent names include Freetrade and Trading 212, with others including X-O, iWeb, eToro, DeGiro, Plus500, etc. I've looked at them in the past and dismissed them. Perhaps I'm a little old-fashioned, but I don't trust something that purports to be free, and I typically dislike the Freemium model as the premium functionality often appears expensive when you dig into it.

The more traditional route is with Barclays Bank, Hargreaves Lansdown (HL), Halifax Bank, Fidelity, AJ Bell, Charles Stanley, etc. I use the first two. I highly rate the user experience, and I think the costs are reasonable for the service I receive.

Whichever provider you select to trade through, you need to be aware of the various fees, you should check review sites for other users experiences, and you should check that the Financial Conduct Authority regulates them and that your customer funds are protected by the Financial Services Compensation Scheme, which protects you up to £85,000 should the company go bust.

Fees

The total costs that you incur over a year of trading will include:

- **Annual account fees** - these vary by provider, from a flat fee per month to a percentage of your investment holdings.

  Barclays charge 0.2% on funds and 0.1% on shares, across all accounts, with a minimum charge of £4 per month and a maximum of £125 per month.

  HL charges are more complicated. There's no charge for holding shares in their Fund & Share Account, but funds are charged at 0.45% reducing in increments after £250k. Shares held in an ISA are charged at 0.45%, but capped at £45 per year.

*   **Trading charges** - these vary by provider. As noted earlier, some apps advertise this as being free.

    I mainly trade through Barclays Bank at £6 per trade for shares and £3 per trade for funds. While I don't use it, they only charge £1 per trade for regular automated investments, which might interest some people.

    When I use my Hargreaves Lansdown account, they charge up to £11.95 per share trade (this reduces based on trading volume). They do not charge for buying or selling funds.

*   **Stamp Duty** - this is a government levy at 0.5% on the amount of your purchase.

*   **PTM levy** - this is a £1 levy for transactions above £10,000 which goes to the Panel of Takeovers and Mergers.

*   **Currency Exchange** - some platforms allow you to trade in non sterling stocks, and will charge a conversion fee. I have never encountered this, as I only trade in UK listed companies.

For example, I invested £10,000 and ticked the box to include fees, I paid 103.01 pence per share, and the deal showed that I had purchased 9,653 shares for £9,943.96. The trading charge was £6, and the Stamp Duty was £49.72. The total cost was £9,999.68.

I sold all the shares at 108.77 pence per share, and the deal showed that it was worth £10,499.20. The trading charge was £6, and because the transaction was over £10,000, there was a PTM levy of £1. The cash I received was £10,492.20.

So I paid out £49.72 in Stamp Duty, £12 in trading charges, and £1 to the Panel of Takeovers and Mergers, a total cost of £62.72. In this example, the costs equated to 0.65 pence per share (£62.72p, so 6272 pence divided by 9,653 shares), so I needed the shares to increase by more than 1p to cover my costs and make some money.

As the shares had increased 5.7p when I sold, I made £492, which was nearly a 5% return on my investment. I also incurred a monthly account fee, but I was still a happy customer based on my multiple trades throughout the month.

Barclays Bank also has a Barclays Price Improver, which, when I'm using the 'Quote and Deal' function, often shows my trades execute at a slightly better price.

Costs and tax efficiency

If you are only looking to invest a small amount it may be better to invest outside an ISA, as your dividends and gains are likely to be less than your annual allowances, and therefore tax-free.

If you invest in a tax-free ISA, which keeps your income from dividends and capital gains tax-free regardless of your personal allowances, you may incur platform costs – for example, FreeTrade provides a free to use general investment account but charges a flat fee of £3 per month for their ISA account.

For getting started with a low investment, you might save money by sticking to a free general trading account.

‼ WARNING ‼

When I looked at Freetrade, their complete share dealing offering was a premium package costing £9.99 per month. When I looked at Trading 212, it was hard to see where they made their money – everyone needs to make money, it's how the platforms get developed and supported – so I did an internet search, and the results were fascinating. A Financial Times article was notably candid, entitled *"When commission-free trading isn't (really) free".* I also used TrustPilot (https://uk.trustpilot.com) to see what users have been saying.

A typical approach seems to be a "bait and switch" strategy. They get you signed up and then start marketing other products to you that they do make money on. Some platforms even make it so seamless between products that it would be easy to make a mistake. The most lucrative products are Contracts For Difference (CFDs). When I looked at the Trading 212 CFD offering, there was a warning in small print at the top of the screen that said:

"CFDs are complex instruments and come with a high risk of losing money rapidly due to leverage. 76% of retail investor accounts lose money when trading CFDs with this provider. You should consider whether you understand how CFDs work and whether you can afford to take the high risk of losing your money".

So with 76% of retail investors, that being you and me, losing money on CFDs, I can now see where they make their money!

Some apps or platforms offer a 'Copy Trading' functionality, so you can mirror what others do – this also seems high risk, and you could also be getting into CFDs again.

Lots of the free trading apps offer CFD trading, currency trading, Crypto-currency, and other offerings. I've avoided these as they appear high risk. I like to Keep It Simple, so I'll stick to buying a share, holding it, and selling it when I decide to sell it! Safe and steady, it's worked for me!

PART TWO:
Investing and Trading in Shares

On reflection:

"Just because you can, doesn't mean you should"

"Fail fast, and live to fight another day"

"When you use a wooden fire poker, you might get your fingers burnt"

CHAPTER 6

Investment Ground Rules

Ground Rules

As I tell my kids, they can make their own decisions ... BUT, they might like to consider adopting some, or all, of these ground rules:

#1 – do your research and plan your prices. Your investment can wait. Something too good to miss and needs instant action is often too good to be true!

#2 - never invest any cash that you can't afford to do without – don't use cash that you've set aside for rent, food, bills, etc. – if the share price falls, you may need to sell the shares at a loss.

#3 – start small, don't be greedy. Build your confidence and experience the ups and downs of the stock market without risking more than you are comfortable losing.

#4 – keep it simple, keep it low risk. Look at the shares in the FTSE 100 and FTSE 250, and start your learning by investing in some of those that you like.

#5 - avoid everything you don't understand. If you don't know what the company does and how it makes money, don't invest in it.

#6 - avoid the higher risk stocks on the AIM market and the FTSE Small Caps. These are something for later in your learning curve.

#7 - avoid the 'get rich quick' higher-risk trading activities such as CFD's (Contracts For Difference), Foreign Exchange/Currency trading, Cryptocurrency, etc. You are more likely to lose all your money on these.

#8 - avoid the commodities market unless you know a lot about the global supply and demand of silver, gold, palladium, platinum, oil, etc

#9 – spread your risk, so parcel up your investments into several companies, don't have 'all your eggs in one basket' as the saying goes! Ideally, make sure these companies are all in different sectors to help spread your risk. Investing in three banking stocks does not reduce your risk of events impacting the banking sector!

#10 – avoid Initial Public Offerings (IPO's), there's often a lot of hype, and everyone thinks it's a license to print money – it isn't. Just look at the Deliveroo IPO as an example! Take particular care if the business was previously supported by Private Equity (PE) investors. The IPO is their exit, often earning them very attractive multiples of their investment. Many PE investors load the company with excessive debt, drive down costs and delay necessary spending – beware, or simply stay clear!

#11 – do not copy trade! Some platforms allow you to follow other traders, it's a great way for them to generate business, and you don't need to do anything … and that's a huge risk! You won't have done any research, you are likely to be buying at a higher price than the person you are following, and your attitudes to risk could be completely different!

#12 – do not buy more of an under-performing share. This is called averaging down when your share prices are falling, don't do it - you are only increasing your risk into one company. Keep invested across several shares, or ideally use this spare cash to invest into funds instead!

#13 - try it out without actually committing your cash. Decide on the shares. Use your trading app to get a price. Note the share price, then follow it for a few days or weeks. Could you have made some money from it rising in price, or would you still be holding at a loss?

#14 – be prepared to be holding less value than you invested! This happens immediately on purchase, as you incur stamp duty and dealing costs. Still, markets can be volatile, and it only takes some negative news or negative sentiment in the US market for prices to fall, followed by the UK and European markets!

#15 – learn to 'kill your interest'. When I do research, I will quickly 'kill my interest' in a company when I read or interpret the following things:

- The company is loss-making but has excellent prospects and will make a profit in the future. Yep, right – that's like saying my wife will stop buying more clothes because the wardrobe is full. Nope, not going to happen!

- The company has issued a profit warning, ach, bad news, skip, move on.

- The dividends are canceled or are lower than expected (unless you're in the middle of a global pandemic, in which case that looks pretty sensible, to be fair!)

- The company has delayed filing company accounts – mmm, that's not excellent management, planning, or communication, something is wrong – skip, move on.

- The company has high net debt levels. You need to gauge what is high – the more research you do, the better you become at thinking, 'wow, that's not good!'

- The company has a very high PE ratio, which suggests it might be over-valued. I don't use EPS or PE for decisions, but I don't like racy PE's.

- Anything about investigations or director suspensions, fraud investigations, etc. Skip, move on.

- Anything about a 'hole in the accounts', oops, skip, move on!

- Directors have sold their shares, mmm, skip, move on!

- Lots of 'hype' – yep, I don't like fluff and marketing spin, so anything coming across with a sales spin … bin it, move on.

Follow these rules, and you increase your chances of long-term success – good luck!

CHAPTER 7

Selecting Shares

This chapter covers the free research tools I use and how I identify companies to research and possibly invest.

Free research

The internet is full of advice and information, often leading to a subscription to pay for the service! I've managed adequately well without any subscription services. My preferred sources of free information are:

News app on my phone – the channels and topics I've selected to follow include Times Money Mentor, Reuters UK, Proactive, Yahoo Finance UK, Financial Markets, Stock Markets, Business, Business Insider, BBC News, SKY News, The Times, and The Sunday Times, MarketWatch, Evening Standard, iNews, etc. These provide plenty of thought and inspiration!

Stock app on my phone - I have the FTSE 100 index, FTSE 250 index, and the companies that I follow just a click away. Take care selecting the correct stock - for example, searching for CRH shows a result for CRH NYSE and CRH.L London - it's the London stock that I add to my watchlist. The app also shows top stories, with the Evening Standard articles always being a good read. Interestingly, it also shows some articles that require a subscription on my news app.

London Stock Exchange website - shows you which companies are in each index, their current share price, and movements in pence and percent. I particularly like the Risers, Fallers, and Volume leaders summary. Under the 'Personal Investing' tab, users can set up a free virtual portfolio and watchlist – a great tool to help beginners learn before investing real cash.

Barclays Smart Investor – an online research center provided for free as I have their ISA and Investment products. Loads of interesting information, easily accessed - it looks a little like the London Stock Exchange data – but with the added value of latest share news, market news, broker roundup, broker ratings, weekend share tips, fund news, company factsheets, etc. They also provide an email summary, 'Views on the news'.

Hargreaves Lansdown – a particularly easy-to-follow online research center, provided for free as I have my SIPP and Investment Account with them. The information includes most viewed shares today, buy/sell ratios of leading shares, stock market news, company news, share tips, latest share research. They also have a free app, which seems to provide all that great News and Market information, including broker tips and share tips, for free. By signing into your account on the app, you get access to the 'real-time' share prices feature.

FreeTrade – I use the FreeTrade app to keep a watchlist. It's quick to open the app and check the prices, which are only a few minutes behind real-time. I also signed up for their 'Honey by Freetrade' email news updates.

Dividends – If you search for "Dividend data UK" you'll find the website www.dividenddata.co.uk. It lists out the UK listed company announced dividends, ex-dividend dates, and dividend payment dates, and rather nicely, it also provides the current share price and the calculated dividend yield. It's an excellent summary to review and get ideas for research targets.

In the News

Reading about companies in the news can be thought provoking. Headlines can cause panic, and opportunity. Imagine reading the news on Friday 9th April and seeing:

"Tui slumped after the travel company said it was raising up to Euro 400m (£348m) by selling convertible bonds to strengthen its finances during continuing travel restrictions caused by the Covid-19 crisis."

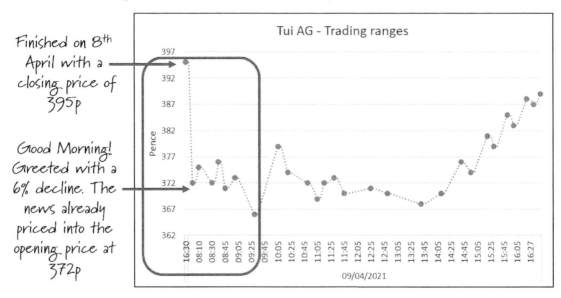

Finished on 8th April with a closing price of 395p

Good Morning! Greeted with a 6% decline. The news already priced into the opening price at 372p

Tui AG - Trading ranges

09/04/2021

The Tui shares had closed Thursday afternoon at 395p, opened 6% lower near 372p on the Friday … then reaction to this news sent the share price down to 366p by 9.30 am, down 29p (8%) against the previous day's closing price!

The shares rallied up to 379.34p by 10 am, falling back to 367.6p by 1.40 pm… then spent the rest of the afternoon heading back upwards, to close at 389p – just 6p (1.5%) down against the Thursday close!

My share price graphs are a representation. I've only taken a selection of highs and lows for illustration purposes. The actual trading charts are far busier!

The news motivated selling. Having traded around the opening price through the morning, the afternoon shows demand picked up, and the share price rallied back towards the previous day's close.

To understand Tui, you need to do your research, look back at pre-pandemic trends, look at the pandemic support they've received, their increased debt position, and consider the global vaccination news, expected return to travel for business, and holidays, etc. After the collapse of Monarch and Thomas Cook, airlines look high risk! I already hold some underperforming Tui shares, so I was not going to add any more.

On the same morning, I read a Reuters news headline:

> *"Lookers jumped 14.1% after the auto retailer forecast 2021 underlying profit before tax to be materially ahead of analysts' estimates."*

I had a look at their share price graph, and the shares hit a 55p ceiling on 1st, 60p ceiling on 6th, 63p on the 7th, then jumped to 71p on the 8th following this announcement. The 8p movement, from 63p to 71p is 12.7% - so the headline is close.

I thought it might be a good target to place a 'limit order' to buy around 65-66p if the price fell back from profit-taking. More research needed.

Found it was listed in the FTSE 250, so happy it wasn't AIM or small-cap.

Found that shares had been suspended due to a £19m hole in the accounts, and investigation by the FCA into their 2017 and 2018 results – that was enough for me, binned.

Headlines can also cause joy and excitement. Imagine seeing:

> *"Global recruitment firm Page Group jumped 10.8% to the top of the mid-*

cap index on higher 2021 profit outlook."

This is a post-pandemic reaction, as this jump in share price resulted from reporting a 2% increase in first-quarter profits!

Looking back to the 1st April, the shares opened at 471.6p and gradually climbed to 500p by the close on Thursday 8th April.

This article was priced into the opening price of 530.5p on Friday 9th April, up 30.5p (6.1%) against the previous days close, peaking at 556p by 8.54 am, then trading in the range of 540-555p during the rest of the day, closing at 555p, up 55p (11%) against the Thursday close.

Best to read this news and add it to your watchlist. It's also interesting to watch how news impacts the sector. Hays is another listed recruitment firm that was trading at 157.6p by the close of Thursday 8th April and opened at 162.1p on the Friday morning – up 4.5p (2.9%) against the night before. Hays had a quick rally to peak at 167.1p by 8.06 am, up 10p (6.3%) against the night before, before slipping back and trading in the range 162-165p and closing at 162.2p back near where it opened ... which was still 3% up on the day before!

Broker views

Every listed company will have an appointed 'house' broker – these brokers and analysts will publish reports on their clients and other listed companies. They often work closely with the business, attempting to get a feel for their modeling assumptions on the various components of the business – often using complex spreadsheet models. Any change in these assumptions will impact the company valuation, and therefore the expected share price.

If you sign up to the email briefings and news or review the websites mentioned for research, you might see headlines like these – being examples from Friday 9th April:

"Britain's biggest sportswear retailer JD Sports Fashion added 1.3% after Berenberg raised its price target on the stock."

"Shares in British American Tobacco declined 2.5% to the bottom of the index after J.P. Morgan downgraded the stock to 'Neutral' from 'Overweight.'"

"Funeral services provider Dignity plc fell 1.9% after Peel Hunt downgraded the stock to 'Sell' in light of positive momentum of vaccines."

As with any news, you need to research the company and follow the share price graphs for that day, and after that, it takes time, but that's how you learn.

The Dignity share price graph was interesting. The shares closed Thursday 8th April at 654p, then opened 25.5p (3.9%) lower at 628.5p after this broker update. Prices bounced around a lot, and by mid-afternoon, had exceeded the previous day's close.

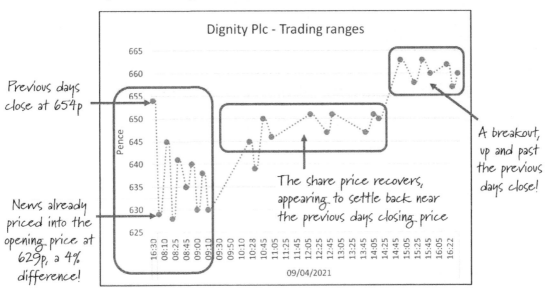

So while the broker downgraded to a 'sell', it looks like that upset the share price for the first hour, then there must have been consistent buying to start pushing the price back up and past the previous day's close! The lesson being, don't take a broker's recommendation as anything more than a view – this 'sell' guidance could have sent the share price into a downward spiral, so interesting to see it had the opposite effect!

Share tips

Ok, I can't think of any share tip that I've read and invested immediately ... not since my younger days, when I followed share tips and lost money on AIM! I also keep away from social media and bulletin boards – I use the news, broker ratings, and share tips as nudges towards some research. I'll often see something that 'kills my interest', and I move on.

Take care with share tips, be suspicious rather than motivated to buy. To get started, note the company name, do your research, follow the share price graphs and learn some lessons without investing your cash.

I skimmed through the Hargreaves Lansdown app on 12th April and stopped on their article entitled *'Five shares to Watch first quarter update'*, dated as '4 days ago' – so possibly released on 8th April. One share discussed was Ibstock, which I traded during the lockdown, with a comment:

"Demand for the group's brick and concrete products has recovered faster than management initially expected. With house sales and prices remaining robust in the early months of 2021, we think the outlook for long-term demand for Ibstock's products is good."

As a few days had already passed, I had a look at their share price graph to see the impact of this positive article ... the shares had hit peaks of 225-226p four times since the start of April, being the resistance or ceiling level – then this article potentially increased demand for the shares, which helped the shares break through and hit a new ceiling of 229p by lunch on 12th April.

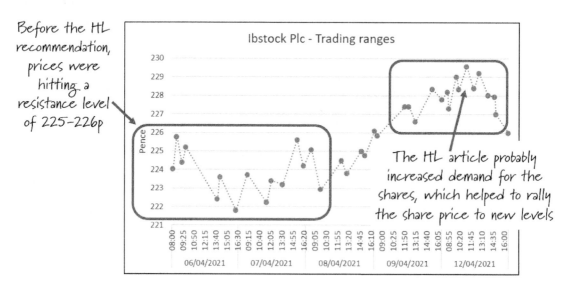

Before the HL recommendation, prices were hitting a resistance level of 225-226p

The HL article probably increased demand for the shares, which helped to rally the share price to new levels

While the shares fell back to 226p at the close, a new resistance level of 229-230p appeared over the following days. Interestingly, there was a global stock market crash on 21st April, which knocked the stock to a low of 219.7p, before it bounced back to another new high at 233p on 26th April. We cover market events as being buying opportunities later!

Initial Public Offerings (IPOs)

There's a common misconception that new share listings are a license to print money, investors rally to buy the shares, and demand pushes the price up, but don't forget the business fundamentals – would it pass your re-search requirements for profit, cash, net debt, dividend record, etc.?

Some have argued that the market conditions were harsh for the Deliv-eroo IPO, but I struggle with their business model. It's another loss-making business promising a great future. I never even shortlisted it as a potential investment!

Despite my lack of interest, around 70,000 individual investors paid 390p per share in the initial public offering. In March 2021, its share price plunged 30% after trading started. I read on 13th April that their shares had hit a new all-time low at 241.7p as selling continued, putting the shares 38% below their IPO price.

Don't entirely dismiss IPO's. Some may be worth having a look at – but you need to do your research.

Fund research

An effortless way to identify good companies is by researching funds – which we cover in Part 3. They always quote their top 10 investments and percentage holdings, so you can assume professionals have shortlisted them after thorough research and that they have a top 10 holding as they expect the stock to deliver good returns.

If you want to build your own portfolio of shares, it's an excellent place to get ideas – then go and do your research and make sure you are happy with your selection.

CHAPTER 8

Trading in Shares

Do you want to trade in shares? Buying low and selling high regularly? If so, this chapter will help – but recognize that it takes a lot more of your time, and can wreck your nerves!

I enjoy the fun of trading - selling and making a profit is very satisfying ... but it's a waiting game. The shares can go lower or bounce around your purchase price for days, then you miss the rally, and they're back to your purchase price again.

Selecting shares for trading

For trading, you need to pick volatile shares, where the share price moves regularly enough for you to buy and sell to make regular profits. I look for at least a 3% movement between the peaks and troughs, as those numbers regularly work for me.

I like to look at share price graphs on my phone's Stock app - I review the day, week, and one-month trends to identify a pattern in the ups and downs, looking for a regular 3% gap between the support and resistance levels. This is quite hard, as share prices on my watch list range from Lloyds Bank at 45p to AstraZeneca at £77.15p – so a little spreadsheet template helps Keep It Simple (see below).

I don't follow the day trading approach, where you buy and sell the same day. Day traders might typically be investing in riskier gambles, so they don't want to have cash tied up overnight or on weekends.

I like to think that I've lowered my risk, as I now only trade in the FTSE 100 and sometimes the FTSE 250 market, and I only trade in shares that I'm willing to hold for longer should the price decline below my purchase price. I typically only look for a 3% movement, so I often jump out while the share price might continue to rise – whenever I hold out for more, I seem to miss out.

A real-life example

For trading shares, I use 'limit order' from my app's drop-down list. This allows me to set the price I want to buy or sell, and the deal is triggered automatically when the share price is at that level or better. We cover the various buying options later.

Let's work through a real example from my recent trading, using Barclays Bank Plc as the example. The chart shows the prominent highs and lows during a week in early April. You can see a pattern of resistance – that ceiling price at which profit-taking brings the price back down, and the support – that floor price at which buying rallies the share price again. I took this range as being around 184p to buy and 190p to sell.

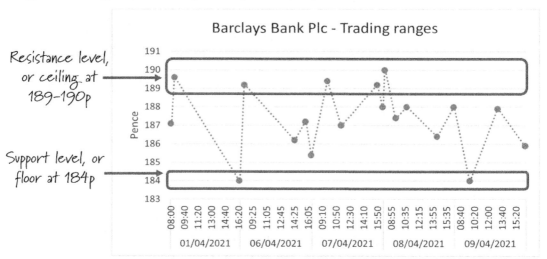

On the 8th April 2021, I placed a 'limit order' at 185p that triggered buying 10,755 shares at 184.7963p for a total cost of £19,981.22.

The 13th, 15th, and 16th April offered sell opportunities at the 190p level, so I placed a 'limit order' to sell at 190p, which triggered and achieved 190.002p with proceeds of £20,427.72 after costs. Having held for eight days, I made a tax-free profit of £446.50 in my ISA, being a 2.2% return.

Both the buy and sell trades were automated, using the 'limit order' option, and the target prices were based on my view of the support and resistance levels that week – very nice!

How much should I invest?

To illustrate trading gains and different levels of investment, we need to step back to the share price graph. The chart showed the support level around 184p and the resistance around 190p.

When I typed those into my spreadsheet template, it showed that the 6p gain on 184p was a 3.3% increase.

	A	B	C
1	Resistance level (ceiling)	190	
2			
3	Support level (floor)	184	
4			
5	Difference	6	3.3%
6			

As the price range provides a 3.3% return, we'll use my target selling price of plus 3% to first illustrate how much can be gained from a single investment.

Each trade consists of two lines, a buy line and a sell line. I've also added the price difference between the share prices as a reminder.

C	D	E	F	G	H	I	J	K	L	M	N
					Deal	PTM	Stamp	Buy	Sell		
Type	Notes	Share Price	Qty	Total Value	Cost	Levy	Duty	Cost	Receipt	Profit	% gain
Buy	£1k @ Target buy	184	537	988.08	6		4.94	999.02			
Sell	Target sell, at +3%	189.52	537	1,017.72	6				1,011.72	13	1.3%
		5.52									
Buy	£3k @ Target buy	184	1,619	2,978.96	6		14.89	2,999.85			
Sell	Target sell, at +3%	189.52	1,619	3,068.33	6				3,062.33	62	2.1%
		5.52									
Buy	£5k @ Target buy	184	2,700	4,968.00	6		24.84	4,998.84			
Sell	Target sell, at +3%	189.52	2,700	5,117.04	6				5,111.04	112	2.2%
		5.52									

This analysis shows that a £1k investment (£1,000) could buy 537 shares at 184p each, costing £999.02p after stamp duty and dealing fees. Selling at a price 3% higher, at 189.5p, would deliver a profit of £13 after dealing fees.

A £3k investment buys more shares and would deliver a profit of £62, while a £5k investment would deliver a profit of £112.

If you have more significant amounts to invest, the profits ratchet up nicely. The analysis shows that £10k would buy 5,404 shares at 184p, costing £9,999.08 after stamp duty and dealing costs. The 3% price increase to 189.5p takes the holding over £10,000, so a further £1 fee is charged on disposal for the PTM levy, making a profit after costs of £236.

	C	D	E	F	G	H	I	J	K	L	M	N
						Deal	PTM	Stamp	Buy	Sell		
	Type	Notes	Share Price	Qty	Total Value	Cost	Levy	Duty	Cost	Receipt	Profit	% gain
	Buy	£10k @ Target buy	184	5,404	9,943.36	6		49.72	9,999.08			
	Sell	Target sell, at +3%	189.52	5,404	10,241.66	6	1			10,234.66	236	2.4%
			5.52									
	Buy	£30k @ Target buy	184	16,219	29,842.96	6	1	149.21	29,999.17			
	Sell	Target sell, at +3%	189.52	16,219	30,738.25	6	1			30,731.25	732	2.4%
			5.52									
	Buy	£50k @ Target buy	184	27,034	49,742.56	6	1	248.71	49,998.27			
	Sell	Target sell, at +3%	189.52	27,034	51,234.84	6	1			51,227.84	1,230	2.5%
			5.52									

A £30k investment makes a profit of £732, while a £50k investment makes a profit of £1,230.

These profits are actually capital gains and are free from tax if traded in an ISA account. If trading in a general investment account, they are taxable if they exceed your capital gains tax allowance of £12,300 for 2021/22.

Clearly, the more you invest, the more you can make – smaller investments have a lot of the gain taken up in dealing costs. If you used a free-trading app to save the £12 of dealing fees on the £1,000 trade, the profit would nearly double from £13 to £25.

I've tried this using the FreeTrade app, but without paying for the premium functionality, you would have to be monitoring the share prices all day, every day, to catch the target buy and sell prices. You would need the FreeTrade premium package to access their 'limit order' functionality.

Cumulative trading

While the profit from one trade can be attractive, reinvesting the profits into the next trade makes it even nicer – this is about making money on the previous gains, this is called the compounding effect.

This example illustrates six trades, starting with an initial £10k investment making a profit of £236. This profit is added to the next investment, so by the sixth investment, £11.2k is being invested, and it achieves a profit of £265. The total profits from the six trades are £1.5k, being an attractive 15% return.

Type	Notes	Share Price (p)	Qty	Total Value	Deal Cost	PTM Levy	Stamp Duty	Buy Cost	Sell Receipt	Gain £	Gain %	Cash Balance
Buy	£10k @ Target buy	184	5,404	9,943.36	6		49.72	9,999.08				0.92
Sell	Target sell, at +3%	189.52	5,404	10,241.66	6	1			10,234.66	235.58	2.36%	10,235.58
Buy	£10.2k @ Target buy	184	5,531	10,177.04	6	1	50.89	10,234.93				0.66
Sell	Target sell, at +3%	189.52	5,531	10,482.35	6	1			10,475.35	240.43	2.35%	10,476.01
Buy	£10.4k @ Target buy	184	5,661	10,416.24	6	1	52.08	10,475.32				0.69
Sell	Target sell, at +3%	189.52	5,661	10,728.73	6	1			10,721.73	246.41	2.35%	10,722.42
Buy	£10.7k @ Target buy	184	5,794	10,660.96	6	1	53.30	10,721.26				1.15
Sell	Target sell, at +3%	189.52	5,794	10,980.79	6	1			10,973.79	252.52	2.36%	10,974.94
Buy	£10.9k @ Target buy	184	5,931	10,913.04	6	1	54.57	10,974.61				0.33
Sell	Target sell, at +3%	189.52	5,931	11,240.43	6	1			11,233.43	258.83	2.36%	11,233.77
Buy	£11.2k @ Target buy	184	6,071	11,170.64	6	1	55.85	11,233.49				0.27
Sell	Target sell, at +3%	189.52	6,071	11,505.76	6	1			11,498.76	265.27	2.36%	11,499.03

Capital gain from 6 trades, achieving a 3% price increase	1,499.03
Percentage gain	15.0%

The illustration above shows that while the selling price is 3% higher than the purchase price, the stamp duty and dealing costs reduce the profit, creating a percentage gain of 2.36% on each trade.

We can simply calculate the projected profits by using this 2.36% as the return on each trade, as illustrated below:

	Brought Forward (£)	2.36% Gain (£)	Carried Forward (£)
Opening balance			**10,000**
Trade 1	10,000	236	10,236
Trade 2	10,236	242	10,478
Trade 3	10,478	247	10,725
Trade 4	10,725	253	10,978
Trade 5	10,978	259	11,237
Trade 6	11,237	265	11,502
Trade 7	11,502	271	11,774
Trade 8	11,774	278	12,052
Trade 9	12,052	284	12,336
Trade 10	12,336	291	12,627
Trade 11	12,627	298	12,925
Trade 12	12,925	305	**13,230**
		Total gains	**3,230**
		Percentage gain	**32.3%**

The illustration shows the initial £10k investment building to £11.5k after the sixth trade, as demonstrated earlier, but it goes on to show an additional six trades with each one investing the earlier profits.

So starting the year with a £10k trading 'pot', managing one trade per month and selling at 3% above the purchase price, reinvesting the profits on each trade – after 12 trades, the £10k 'pot' would have increased to £13.2k – achieving total gains of £3.2k, being a 32% return.

If you had £20k to invest in a tax-free ISA and used the £20k plus gains for trading, that gain would be double – so an increase of £6.4k, being 32% of £20k.

Likewise, if you had £100k invested in an ISA and used that and the gains for trading, achieving a 32% return generates a tax-free profit of £32k for the year!

This demonstrates why picking a stock with just a 3% volatility, watching the support and resistance levels, then placing 'limit order' trades to buy and sell at those prices on a regular basis can be an effective trading strategy.

!!!Warning!!!

Before you get too excited, consider that your entire investment could be tied up achieving nothing if the market price fell away. The number of trades you could make is partly down to luck and timing. You could buy and sell five times in a week, or just once in a month, or you could go months waiting for the price to recover enough to sell and get your cash out!

CHAPTER 9

Investing in Shares

Instead of trading, do you want to Invest in shares – so buy and hold?

I start with a good dividend yield, then look for upside growth potential – reinvesting the dividend income back into buying more of the stock. If I can see a 10% return for the year, I'm happy, but I really want it to be 20% plus.

How much should I invest?

If you have less than £1,000 to invest, save up – wait for a little!

If you have £1,000 to invest, learn with one stock – build some experience.

If you have £3,000 to invest, consider splitting that into three investments of £1,000.

If you have £9,000 to invest, consider splitting that into three investments of £3,000.

If you have £20,000 to invest, consider splitting that into four investments of £5,000.

I think you get my message. It's how I parcel up my investments.

Before you invest in shares, though, spend some time considering whether you would be better investing in funds instead – we cover funds in Part 3.

Investment returns

Investment returns come in three forms. You have the dividends a company pays out to shareholders, the share price growth (hopefully), and some company's offer shareholder rewards.

If you select shares to buy and hold, consider each of those three returns as areas to research. Once you've done the research and become an investor, you may then sit back and ride the ups and downs of the stock market. Investments are multiple-year strategies where you believe in long-term value and growth.

Invest for dividends

You'll frequently see company announcements and news about dividends, but it's not immediately apparent if that's a good return or not. You need to divide the dividend by the current share price, making sure both are either in pence or pound and pence - so either 9/180, or 0.09/1.80 – that's your dividend yield. Both these examples equal 0.05, which you multiply by 100 to get the percentage, being 5%.

An alternative to investing in shares is investing the cash in a bank account to earn interest. With such low interest rates at the moment, it's not hard to do better on dividends and share price growth. However, unlike your 'safe' cash in a bank account, cash tied up in shares can go down in value or be lost entirely.

There's no point investing in a company with a large dividend if your investment goes down in value. You need your investment to be growing in value – so that's where research is essential.

That website I mentioned in the Research section is an excellent place to start, but make sure to confirm the data by checking the company's website.

Note - if you search 'Aviva', you will get their website aimed at customers. You need to search 'Aviva plc investor relations' and find their website that provides sections such as investors, newsroom, shareholder services, dividends, etc. This is the same for most listed companies.

I've used my savings outside the ISA, in the Investment Account, to invest in good dividend payers, as it's nice to use up the government's annual tax-free allowance of £2,000 – it's there, so I might as well plan to use it!

A little dividend example

Back to the Aviva news article that I read on 4th March entitled:

 "Aviva eyes cash handouts after a record year in savings and retirements."

The 14 pence per share dividend sounded attractive, and the company prospects under the new Chief Executive looked promising. I checked out the share price and was able to buy at 388.534p, making the dividend yield 3.6%. I thought this looked like an attractive dividend yield, with an upside for further dividends and share price growth - so I was happy to invest and hold.

As it happened, I decided to sell on 4th May, just two months later. The shares were at 401.2p, which made 12.67p per share, a 3.3% increase on my purchase price. After costs, the net capital gain was 2.7%. Add on the 3.6% yield from the dividends, and that two-month investment provided a total return of 6.3%.

If you'd invested £10k, the 6.3% return would have generated a gain of £630. If done through an ISA, both the dividends and the capital gain would also be tax-free.

Another dividend example

On 12th April, I read this Hargreaves Lansdown (HL) broker roundup:

> *"Legal & General – Barclays reiterates overweight with a target price of 351p."*

Remember, overweight means to hold more in relation to other stocks, so it's a positive review.

I initially ignored it, as I was already invested in Aviva and didn't want to be holding two insurance giants, but a little research changed my mind...

With the shares going ex-div on the Thursday of that week, the dividend of 12.64p was still showing an attractive 4.3% yield against a price of 296.2p.

I looked at the week's trading, and four peaks were ranging from 298.1 to 298.6p, with lows of 293.5p, 295.1p, and 294p.

As the markets opened on Tuesday 13th April, the opening buy price was 297p, and by 10 am was at 298.5p – so not wanting to buy at the previous peaks (resistance level), I placed a limit order at 293p – not expecting to buy-in. Amazingly, the shares hit a high of 299.2p, then started to fall back to 294.3p by 4.30 pm. At 8 am on Wednesday, 14th April, my limit order was completed for 292.969p.

Had I done a 'quote and deal' and paid around 298.5p, that would have been 5.5p and 1.9% more than what I achieved by waiting - that's already a great start!

With the current year's £20k ISA allowance invested in 6,790 L&G shares on the day before they go ex-div, that guaranteed a tax-free dividend of £858. An attractive 4.3% return, but only if I sell at my purchase price. I will hold onto the shares to see how they perform above the 293p – as the broker target price of 351p looks a long way away!

As expected, the shares dropped by the value of the dividend on XD day, and hit lows of 268p during April. They have since recovered to 281p in early May – so they still show as loss-making in my portfolio!

Invest for growth

This is a multiple-year strategy. It's often said that those who regularly invest for the long term achieve higher returns than those that trade in and out. That might be the case, but after being burnt in the past, I've decided to leave most of my investing for growth to funds, which I cover later in this book. It just seems easier, simpler, and lower risk.

Investing and holding shares means buying with confidence, backing your decision, and sticking out the highs and the lows.

To start, you can look at the economy. History shows a cycle of economic growth and decline, boom and bust. Assessing where we are now and where we are heading, you might identify what companies should do well.

You'll frequently read articles that refer to cyclical shares or defensive shares. Cyclical shares typically perform well when the economy is growing, as they mirror the health of the economy, doing well in good times and less well in tough times. Sectors include Travel & Leisure, Retail, Construction, Property, Manufacturing, Engineering, Banks, etc.

Defensive shares typically perform better during a downturn. They include Household Goods, Food & Beverages, Pharmaceuticals, Support Services, Utilities, Life Insurance, etc

Look for profitable businesses with products and services that are always in demand.

While cyclical and defensive sectors are one way to look at the future, you should also look at how the world is changing. Technology has moved at a massive pace, online shopping shot up with the Covid-19 pandemic, legislation is moving us towards electric vehicles, renewables energy is on the green agenda, 3D printing, Artificial Intelligence, self-driving cars etc., etc. What companies are in this space? What is the next big thing?

Investing in what you know might also work – so companies you know, brands you love.

Why do you shop at a particular supermarket? Do you think they have better customer service, a better selection, higher quality? What makes them stand out ahead of the competition? Have you come across a company through work that you were particularly impressed with?

Invest for shareholder perks?

I thought these were pretty much finished since the extinction of the old paper stock certificates, but I was pleasantly surprised to find a few remain – you might just need your broker involved.

I found similar lists on the Hargreaves Lansdown and Barclays sites by searching "HL shareholder perks" and "Barclay's shareholder perks," respectively, and a much smaller list on the Freetrade site by searching "Freetrade shareholder perks".

Companies offering shareholder perks included Next, Legal & General, Whitbread, Carnival, etc. As an accountant, I'd still have to do a cost-benefit analysis of the costs to buy and hold these shares compared to the value of the perks, but it's still worth having a look!

Diversification

You can lower your risk by spreading investments across several companies, ideally across different sectors and different company sizes, so large-cap and mid-cap. This should theoretically be better than having all your investment in one company or one sector.

From what I can remember about portfolio theory, 60 was the magic number – so 60 different investments is a good diversification of risk – oh well!

Some articles talk of diversification as being across not just shares, but investing in bonds, commodity's and cash, across different countries – capturing international markets, emerging markets, etc.

I like funds for diversifying my risk. Each fund is already a portfolio of different companies. Then my fund choice diversifies globally with a UK fund, European fund, US fund, and an emerging markets fund.

Compounding

It's worth mentioning the impact of compounding. As illustrated in the trading section - whenever you receive a dividend or profit on selling your shares, reinvest what you receive – this increases your future gains even further.

!!!Warning!!!

I think there can be more risk in the investment approach if you are not actively monitoring news, events, etc. This happened to me with some investments I made in 2018, to invest and forget – it didn't work out.

If you want to invest and forget, you might be better off investing in actively managed funds – which we cover in Part 3.

CHAPTER **10**

Buying Shares

This chapter covers the actual process of buying shares, being aware of the market opening hours and technical terms, the various types of purchases you can place, the importance of having a target purchase price in mind, plus using the FreeTrade app and the Barclays Smart Investor app.

Market trading hours

The London Stock Exchange opens for trading at 8.00 am and closes at 4.30 pm. If I want certainty on placing a trade, I use the 'quote and deal' option, so that's during opening hours. I also use 'limit orders' a lot, which can be placed outside opening hours and set for up to 30 days.

Bid and Offer prices

There are usually two values quoted for a share,

- the bid price is the price you can sell at. This will be the lower price

- the offer price is the price at which you can buy. This will be a higher price

This spread between buying and sell prices is common to all trading platforms. It's how the London Stock Exchange's clearinghouse makes its money.

The market prices are constantly changing, so these are only indicative until you get the quote, and even then, the sale or purchase may complete at a slightly different price.

My phone's Stock app displays prices with a 15-minute delay. Some services offer 'real-time' or 'live' prices for a monthly subscription. The Free Trade app opens quickly, and the watchlist displays prices from only a few minutes earlier. If you have a HL account, their app allows you to sign up for real-time prices for free. When you add shares to a watchlist, you can watch the Buy and Sell prices flicker and change every second.

Order type

Buying shares is called placing an order. There are several different types of orders, which can be confusing. Your various options will be set out and explained on your app or platform.

Barclays Smart Investor – order options

Quote and deal – during market opening hours, get a real-time quote available to accept for 15 seconds, so you know the exact price of the buy or sell order. I use this when I want certainty that my buy or sell will be completed.

Limit order – buy or sell at prices set by you, which can be higher or lower than the current market price. You can select how long to keep the order open, from one day to 30 days. The order is monitored automatically until the order expires and will be placed once the set price is reached or exceeded. I use this a lot for trading when I think I've anticipated the floor and ceiling prices, and the share prices are heading in that direction.

Regular Investment – chose to make a repeated purchase of a particular share, fund, or investment trust on a monthly, quarterly, half-yearly, or annual basis.

At Best – these orders can be placed at any time, even if the markets are closed. The order is processed when the market reopens again, at the best price available for the investment and quantity you want to buy or sell.

Stop order or stop-loss - an order to sell an existing shareholding which is triggered if the selling price falls to, or below, a price (the stop price) set by you. I don't use these, but they can provide some protection and help minimize the loss should the share price fall.

Trailing Stop orders – as your share price rises, the trailing stop price also increases, maintaining that gap behind the share price. A sudden drop could trigger the stop loss, but it might allow an exit at a profit rather than at a loss. You could create the same effect by updating your stop loss as the share price rallies.

Share price trends – Target Price

I like share price graphs. I particularly like the daily, weekly, and monthly trends as they are the most recent and can provide a view on the current market views – is there a pattern to the peaks – that resistance level, the ceiling, at which investors sell their shares to take profits, increasing supply and forcing the price down. Is there a pattern to the troughs – that support level, the floor, at which investors get interested again and start buying, increasing demand and raising the price.

After the Covid-19 pandemic, the last twelve-month share price performance is less valuable. It's been a tough year on the market!

Having shortlisted the shares you want to buy, you could just buy them and have done with it … kind of shut your eyes and hope for the best approach … which is what I was probably guilty of many years ago, too excited and just wanting to trade!

I now think it's better to give your intended targets a buy price and a selling price. It helps to frame your thoughts. These target prices should come from your research, the share price graphs, understanding of supply and demand, and your views on the resistance level (ceiling) and support level (floor).

Remember, markets can be affected by a variety of factors. There are loads of things impacting that share price – sometimes the waiting pays off, sometimes you just watch the price rise and wish you'd bought in earlier. As your investing experience increases, your rational decision-making skills may also improve …

Market Opportunities

The more you follow the news, shortlist and follow particular shares, the more often you will see buying opportunities arise – that is, an event unrelated to the company performance that sends a ripple through the global stock markets, and you see shares prices take a tumble.

Week commencing Monday 19th April was such a week. The previous week had closed on a high. The FTSE 100 index had finally broken through the 7,000 level again. Weekend news featured the worsening Covid-19 infections in India and President Biden in the US planning to increase Capital Gains Tax on wealthy individuals. Global sentiment on recovery took a hit.

The US markets tumbled first, then the UK and European markets followed – the FTSE 100 index fell 2%, slipping below the 7,000 level again.

 My phone's stock app showed most of the shares I follow as red downward lines.

This Barclays Bank Plc share price chart shows the impact – the share price fell outside its range for a few days before bouncing back as sentiment improved again. As illustrated on the next chart:

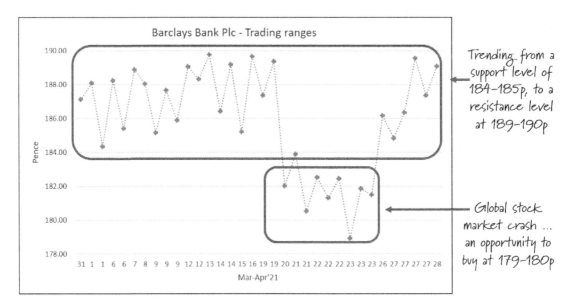

Barclays Bank Plc - Trading ranges

Trending from a support level of 184–185p, to a resistance level at 189–190p

Global stock market crash ... an opportunity to buy at 179–180p

I managed to buy in at 181p – not quite the bottom, but low enough!

I looked at what was going on and took the view that it wasn't fundamentally reducing the value of Barclays Bank. It was market-wide, across the globe.

Following the bank holiday weekend, Tuesday 5th May was another 'global event'. The next day, the Evening Standard reported:

"FTSE 100 set to jump after tumbles yesterday."
"Bizarre stumble which saw tech companies suddenly slide in what some traders were calling a 'flash crash'. The sharp fall was more of a flash wobble, triggered by a large morning slide in Wall Street futures - which indicate how the US markets are going to perform."

The Independent newspaper reported:

"FTSE 100 plunges after a sharp fall in US markets. Comments from US treasury secretary about rising interest rates plunged megacap stocks down."

While Barrons, the US newspaper, reported:

"How Janet Yellen threw the stock market a loop."
"At a conference on Tuesday morning, suggested rates might have to rise."
"After the markets official 4 pm close, she attempted to walk back those earlier remarks. Carefully avoiding any predictions about interest rates and

emphasizing her respect for the central bank's independence.'

My Stock app showed lots of red again, so I noted down the Open, High, Low, and Close prices for a selection of stocks on Tuesday evening. I've then made two comparisons - the closing price versus the high price, and the closing price versus the opening price - as shown below:

	Tuesday 4th May				Close vs High		Close vs Open	
	Open (p)	High (p)	Low (p)	Close (p)	p	%	p	%
FTSE 100	6,969.0	7,034.0	6,912.0	**6,923.0**	-111	**-1.6%**	-46	**-0.7%**
Barclays Plc	177.5	179.5	169.7	**170.9**	-8.6	**-5.0%**	-6.6	**-3.9%**
Lloyds Banking Group Plc	46.1	47.5	45.0	**45.0**	-2.5	**-5.6%**	-1.1	**-2.4%**
AstraZeneca Plc	7,828.0	7,830.0	7,610.0	**7,629.0**	-201	**-2.6%**	-199	**-2.6%**
Diageo Plc	3,252.5	3,304.5	3,237.0	**3,249.0**	-55.5	**-1.7%**	-3.5	**-0.1%**
GlaxoSmithKline Plc	1,338.0	1,352.6	1,331.6	**1,332.2**	-20.4	**-1.5%**	-5.8	**-0.4%**
Unilever Plc	4,247.5	4,269.0	4,195.0	**4,204.0**	-65	**-1.5%**	-43.5	**-1.0%**
Ibstock Plc	224.2	225.4	217.0	**217.0**	-8.4	**-3.9%**	-7.2	**-3.3%**
Aviva Plc	401.8	403.4	393.7	**394.0**	-9.4	**-2.4%**	-7.8	**-2.0%**
Persimmon Plc	3,187.0	3,211.0	3,066.0	**3,074.0**	-137	**-4.5%**	-113	**-3.7%**
Legal & General Group Plc	273.9	276.0	268.9	**270.0**	-6	**-2.2%**	-3.9	**-1.4%**

Many of these stocks had rallied in the morning, then spent the afternoon trending down to close several percent below their opening prices.

It can be difficult to interpret share price movements, as many different factors can be at play. For example, Barclays was being penalized for outstanding quarterly results on the previous Friday, which didn't release any Covid-19 provisions, were not clear on dividend plans, and included higher costs for investment banker bonuses.

Another example is AstraZeneca, which was suffering as the pharmaceutical industry reacted to President Joe Biden's plans to waive patents on Covid-19 vaccines.

Setting those additional issues aside, the share price tumble in the US markets rippled across the pond again, sending our FTSE 100 index and many leading stocks down – losing any gains made in the morning trading before the US awoke.

I took the closing prices on Wednesday evening, which shows how these stocks performed the next day:

	Tuesday 4th May	Wednesday 5th May	Vs Tue close	
	Close (p)	Close (p)	p	%
FTSE 100	6,923.0	7,039.0	116	1.7%
Barclays Plc	170.9	176.7	5.8	3.4%
Lloyds Banking Group Plc	45.0	46.2	1.2	2.7%
AstraZeneca Plc	7,629.0	7,674.0	45	0.6%
Diageo Plc	3,249.0	3,240.0	-9	-0.3%
GlaxoSmithKline Plc	1,332.2	1,339.0	6.8	0.5%
Unilever Plc	4,204.0	4,221.0	17	0.4%
Ibstock Plc	217.0	219.8	2.8	1.3%
Aviva Plc	394.0	403.6	9.6	2.4%
Persimmon Plc	3,074.0	3,128.0	54	1.8%
Legal & General Group Plc	270.0	273.7	3.7	1.4%

The FTSE 100 index bounced back, with some of my watchlist shares doing better than others. Barclays bounced back strongly but was still suffering from the quarterly results reaction, closing at 176.7p compared to the previous highs of 190p. Aviva bounced back nicely, as did Persimmon.

These examples from April and May demonstrate how global events can ripple and impact the UK stock market, creating buying opportunities if you are ready to pounce. Quickly finding and understanding the news behind the issue is vital - you need to conclude whether it is a short-term blip and worth investing in for the rebound or a long-term crash like the March 2020 Covid-19 pandemic ... if in doubt, stay out!

Timing – XD?

If you've done your research, you will know when the shares go ex-dividend. This is important as getting in before the ex-div date means you benefit from receiving the dividend.

On the ex-div date, the shares typically open lower by the value of the dividend – as the company is paying that value out to shareholders who were on the share register before the ex-div date. Seeing this drop in share price can trigger amateur investors to sell the shares, which will lower the price further – don't be one of them!

I monitored the Aviva share prices before and after the dividend, as illustrated in the next chart:

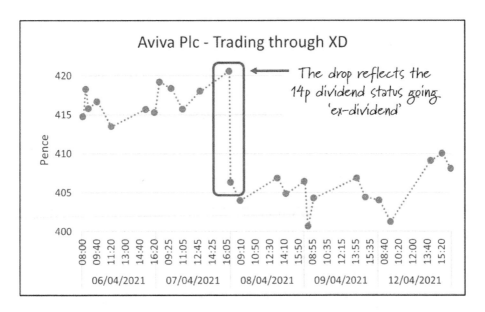

My Aviva Plc chart is an illustration of the key movements. The high of 420.6p was at the close of trading on the day before it went ex-dividend (Ex-Div or XD). The 14p dividend was already priced into the opening price of 406.35p at 8 am on 8th April, being XD day.

Averaging down

This is what happens when you keep buying more, as the share price falls.

Be careful. It's very tempting to think you are buying cheaper and will therefore be averaging your higher buy price with a lower buy price, meaning that the shares won't need to rally as much for you to break even or make a profit ... but what you are doing is increasing your investment 'at risk'. You will now have even more money invested in this company. Step back and think, do you really want to put more cash at risk?

If you're invested in an underperforming company, and the shares have fallen or crashed, sell or hold – do not buy more.

Late to the party?

Don't follow the masses. Whatever is being discussed is in the public domain. We know from the Efficient Market Hypothesis that it is already in the share price. If the share price graph shows that the price has already shot up, you are potentially already too late! Joining at already higher prices is an increased risk and is best avoided.

With social media, there's often a FOMO – a Fear of Missing Out – I just love that acronym, but it reflects what you see and hear nowadays. The Gamestop frenzy in the US was an example of followers piling into the shares at inflated prices. Most of them may lose that money.

Company news is customarily released between 7 am and 8 am, which is the typical approach, so the market will already have that news priced into the opening prices that you see at 8 am – take care, amateur investors might still pile in and buy shares at the higher price – leading to a further rally in the share price and professional investors taking profits, which then results in the share price falling within a day or so. If the good news brought that company onto your radar, do your research, determine your target prices, and buy later when the price comes back down.

Don't get blinkered into following social media and bulletin board activist investor hype, 'insider' news is not really 'insider' – our regulatory environment in the UK makes insider dealing illegal:

"Under the Criminal Justice Act 1993, dealing in securities based on inside information, that is, information that is not yet publicly known and which would affect the price of the securities if it were made public, is a criminal offense in the UK."

Source: https://uk.practicallaw.thomsonreuters.com

What might be put across as 'insider news' on bulletin boards might be an investor, or group of investors, seeking to rally the share price so they can exit and sell their holdings at a profit! Step back, and put what you are reading into perspective. I avoid bulletin boards. I stick to the news and sites I trust – I'll also use review sites like TrustPilot, etc., to read customers' experiences with that business, which can be pretty amusing at times!

Free or cheap trading apps

I've been reluctant to use free or low commission trading apps because I think you get what you pay for. Free often comes with annoying adverts or, in the case of trading apps, lots of articles refer to the 'bait and switch' strategy to get you using other things they can make money on.

For the purpose of this book and someone getting started, I decided to embrace and experience a free app – so at least I could share my observations and experience in comparison to what I'm used to.

I finally shortlisted FreeTrade as it was a Freemium model – so while I'm not a fan of Freemium, I get it – you get the basic functionality for free, then unlock greater functionality with a monthly paid subscription of £9.99 per month.

FreeTrade app

So time to convert thoughts into action and share with you my experience - I downloaded the FreeTrade app and funded my account with £1,000 by setting up the account details in my online banking and making a payment. I hadn't even closed my banking app when I got a FreeTrade notification pop up saying the funds were in my account! I then tested the Fund and Withdraw functionality and withdrew the £1,000 – oops, a message says it takes a few days to reach your account, which they did two days later.

My first frustration with the FreeTrade app was the price display – it showed as £1.88p. I want to see this in pence, not pounds – the £1.88p could be in anywhere in the range of 187.50p to 188.49p – that is fine if you're investing for longer-term, but for trading a small price range, it's not helpful!

My next gripe was just a learning point. I entered £995 to allow some cash for stamp duty – which was unnecessary, as the app takes that into account – so I now know to enter the total cash held value for my next purchase.

I also don't like the share price graph display, as it shows in percentage terms. I want to see the share price graph in actual prices – maybe that's also an option in the premium version.

On a positive note, the FreeTrade app is straightforward to use – I tapped BUY, entered the value, and was given a 'Review order' screen which showed 527 Barclay shares at £1.88, stamp duty of £4.94, total cost estimated at £993.91. I hit 'Confirm Buy,' and it confirmed a purchase of 526 Barclay shares at £1.88, stamp duty of £4.94, and total cost of £993.14

Unlike what I'm used to, there is no quote with the exact price and a 15-second countdown to accept or decline – but it's free, and it will suffice!

To use the limit order functionality, you need to upgrade to the premium version for £9.99 per month, which I think is really needed for trading shares between the support and resistance levels.

The Barclays Smart Investor app

I used to bank and trade with Halifax but then moved to Barclays and found their online trading platform nicer to use. It was a revolution when they launched share trading on their mobile banking app last Summer. I've been able to place trades while picking up my son from Primary School and while sat 100 miles away visiting my mum – the wonders of modern technology!

I like the Smart Investor app, but the current version doesn't have a watch-list function – it's a quick way to review a price and trade – so I've submitted that as a development recommendation! That aside, it is easy to use and has a lot of features that I like.

Unlike the FreeTrade app, which needed a four-digit pin code and then was open and ready to trade, the Barclays app takes a lot more clicks to get to trading - first opening your online banking, then showing all accounts, then selecting the Smart Investor, if you're holding the shares it's quicker to click into the stock and buy more, otherwise you need to click through a search and click the correct stock again - but that's fine for now.

So that's buying shares covered, now let's look at selling shares!

CHAPTER 11

Selling Shares

This chapter looks at the process of selling your shares – whether that's for a profit or a loss – and provides various considerations to your timing.

Self Assessment

If you are trading using an ISA, it's easy, as you don't need to report any of your profits or dividends to HMRC. It's all tax-free. However, if you trade in a general investment account, you will probably need to report the disposals and profits to HMRC through Self Assessment.

While there is an annual exemption of £12,300 (2021/22) for Capital Gains Tax, so any gains up to the level are tax-free, the Self Assessment return still requires those tax-free gains to be reported if the sales proceeds are more than £49,200 (2021/22) – which is easy to exceed when trading shares through the year!

The Self Assessment return provides a 'computation worksheet' for each gain and allows up to 20 worksheets to be submitted. While I view each sales transaction as making a gain, the Self Assessment return notes that disposals of the same share on the same day should be counted as one. The worksheet requires details of the name and type of share (e.g., Barclays Bank Plc, 25p Ords), the quantity disposed of, cost of purchase, incidental costs of the purchase (i.e., dealing costs, stamp duty, PTM levy), total purchase cost, disposal proceeds, incidental costs of the disposal (i.e., dealing costs, PTM levy), net disposal proceeds, and the disposal gain.

As I had more than 20 disposal days, I summarised this into a spreadsheet, saved it as a pdf, and attached the pdf where requested on the form. Even with my tracker spreadsheet of disposals, it was still a lot of admin to present that in the format Self Assessment required.

Knowing this is important (if you are trading outside an ISA), as you can keep life simple by just selling the same number of shares as you purchased. If you are holding shares from, say, three purchases at different prices and decide to go 50:50 and sell half of your holdings, you would need to calculate the average cost of those shares purchased. You would use that average cost to determine the value of shares sold and, therefore, your gain – and that is what you'd have to report via Self Assessment!

I ensure simple traceability by dividing my purchases into 'bundles', which could be bundles of £10k, £20k, etc. When I sell, I often add 2, 3, or more bundles together, so while I may have several transaction costs to buy, I only have one transaction cost to sell. By selling all the shares purchased in those bundles, I ensure simple matching of the quantities, and it means the disposal proceeds can be compared to the sum of each bundle's purchase costs. Nice and neat.

Selecting Sell

If you want to sell shares, you need to open your portfolio, click into the shares you are holding, and select Sell. You will then be prompted to enter the £ value or quantity you want to sell. There's usually a tick box that allows you to 'Sell full investment'.

Order type

Selling shares is also called placing an order. They are the same options for both buying and selling – just make sure you've select Sell.

Market opening hours

You can sell your shares at any time - using 'Best price', 'Stop orders' or 'Limit orders' as noted in the last chapter, but if you want to deal in 'real time', you need to trade during the London Stock Exchange opening hours of 8.00 am to 4.30 pm, using the 'Quote and Deal' option.

Bid and Offer prices

As a reminder from the last chapter, when you look at the share prices, there are usually two values quoted for a share,

- the bid price is the price you can sell at. This will be the lower price

- the offer price is the price at which you can buy. This will be a higher price

Be careful not to start repeating 'buy high, sell low' – while that's correct for the way prices are shown, you don't want that to be your investment mantra ... while it will happen, you need to think the other way around to buy low and sell high to make a profit!

Target Price

If you did your research, you should already have a target selling price in mind.

You'll already have an idea of the price range for trading the peaks and troughs. Combined with what you've read in the news, you'll form a view on whether to sell near the resistance level or hold for a breakout past that resistance level.

Losses

When investments are in loss-making territory – you need to review and make a decision.

As soon as you make a new investment, you are in a loss position. You always get to buy at a higher price than you can sell. You pay 0.5% stamp duty and dealing fees – it looks horrid for a day or two, but it could look like that for weeks, months, or years if the market tumbles away.

If you can salvage some cash by selling at a loss, perhaps it's time to move on and use that cash elsewhere. It's pretty refreshing to sell at a loss, it goes against our human nature and optimism – but it removes that 'ball and chain' and allows your brain to be unleashed.

If you can, revisit your buy decision – do a post-mortem examination and work out what you should have done, with the benefit of hindsight – learn from it, and try not to repeat it!

50:50

Whenever I can't decide, I think going 50:50 always helps. It creates some action. It's a step forward but with fewer consequences, so it's easier to justify and get done!

You could toss a coin in the air, but then it's a 50:50 probability with a 100% buy or sell decision – when I refer to 50:50, I mean you only sell half of your holding – you get to take some profit, and you still have some invested in case the price continues to climb.

Remember about tax reporting. If you hold the shares outside of an ISA, you want to be able to match your disposal quantity to a purchased amount easily. So say you had purchased two bundles at different prices, just sell one bundle – if you sold half of your shares held, you'd have to calculate the average purchase costs.

Taking profits too early

I'm guilty of this, quite significantly guilty during my 2020 pandemic trading! I worked on target prices based on pre-pandemic levels, investing more in those companies with the greatest gap between current trading and returning to pre-pandemic levels. I invested two £20k bundles in Anglo American shares on 31st March 2020 at 1359.60p and on 1st April at 1322.06p. I sold them within a week to make a £1.5k profit ... not hard when the market is recovering ...

As they got closer to the pre-crash 2200p level, I took them off my watchlist. They managed to recover back to pre-Covid levels by November 2020, and they continued to rally, now up 38% against my pre-pandemic target price! ... looking at the shares today on 12th April 2021, had I held onto those two investments and only sold today at 3032p, my profit would have been £50k !!!

I did the same with Barclays bank, pulling out too early – I had a pre-pandemic target price of 170p in mind, so I pulled out at the start of March at 168p. Between the 16th and 22nd March, a new ceiling was tapped three times at 184p, with a floor of 180p. On 23rd March it fell back to 178p but bounced to a new high of 186p the next day. In April, we saw ceilings of 189 to 190 before falling back – so that's 12% past my target!

I should have gone 50:50 and rode the wave higher. Hindsight is a beautiful thing!

The lesson, don't be too eager to take profits – satisfy that urge by selling some, but maybe not all!

Greed?

Watch out for greed. That's the opposite of taking profits too early – it's holding out for more, more, more!

GlaxoSmithKline is a good example. It was trading at the 1800p level pre-pandemic and crashed by 22%, down to 1400p. I traded to the 1550p level making a quick return but didn't buy back in as it was moving up too fast. It reached 1703p by the end of April 2020, and traded in the 1650p range through May and June – anyone holding out for more would have a long wait ahead – the price collapsed again and went down to 1200p by February 2021 – and had only recovered back to the 1350p level by the end of April.

This reinforces the familiar investment warning – your investment may fall in value!

Alternatives?

If you have all your cash invested and have identified some promising alternative companies, you should consider 'weeding out' any slow-moving or 'out of favor' investments - you might be better taking your cash and investing elsewhere, even if that means recognizing a loss.

I did precisely this during the Covid-19 pandemic. I'd shortlisted a dozen companies to follow each day and maintained target prices for buying in – splitting my cash into 'bundles' to trade frequently.

I sold two bundles of Sainsbury's shares at a loss during the pandemic. The share price was moving slower than other options, so after a few weeks, I took a hit of about £1k but freed up my cash to invest elsewhere. On later review of the Sainsbury's share price movements and the gains I made elsewhere, the decision worked out well. That was one of my better decisions!

Sentiment?

DO NOT GET ATTACHED TO YOUR INVESTMENTS! You need to part with them, sometimes at a loss – keeping your investments can be bad for your financial health!

I invested a £10k bundle in Tui shares in January 2020 ... at 984p per share ... having seen a November high of 1081p. We had used them several times for family holidays, another of their competitors had gone bust, prospects looked good, and they had announced a nice dividend, paid in the February of £334.67p – being a 3.3% yield on my investment. But, because I viewed them as a long-term investment, I clearly had my head buried in the sand. The first alarms should have sounded when British Airways announced they were suspending all flights to and from mainland China on 31st January due to the ongoing coronavirus threat. But I didn't think much of it.

By 9th March, the FTSE 100 plunged by more than 8%, its most significant intraday fall since 2008, amid concerns over the spread of Covid-19. Another fall on 12th March was over 10%, the FTSE 100s most significant drop since 1987. On 16th March, Prime Minister Boris Johnson advised everyone in the UK against non-essential travel, and the next day the Tui share price crashed to a low of 284p ... and my £10k investment was now worth less than £3k – so I kept holding, as things could only get better!

Tui's share price peaked on 26th May 2020 at 530p, and I considered getting out with a £5k loss, but I didn't want to lose half my investment, so I held! At the end of April 2021, my portfolio values them at 430.7p per share, worth £4,371p, down a massive 56% ...

I have every confidence that they will recover ... I'm sure holidays will bounce back in 2022, so by 2023 to 2025, the shares might be getting back closer to my original investment ... if their massive amount of debt doesn't take them down or we get hit by another variant of Covid-19, or something else bad happens! So yes, I should have sold and saved you this horror story of my sentiment getting the better of me!

Timing

Check your ex-div dates and decide whether you want to hang in for the potential dividend.

Shares drop by the value of the dividend on the ex-div date, don't panic!

Settlement

When you sell your shares, the disposal proceeds are added to your account balance and are immediately available to reinvest in other purchases. However, if you want to withdraw the proceeds, you will have to wait two to three days until the settlement date. The sales order will generally quote the settlement date.

On settlement day, a withdrawal from my Barclays account takes 20-30 minutes to appear in my current account. The FreeTrade app took two days to appear in my current account.

CHAPTER 12

Spreadsheets

You don't need to be an expert with spreadsheets to use them. This chapter will cover why they are helpful and provide some templates and formula's to help you get started.

If you are already a spreadsheet wizard, please skip this chapter – as you have probably already built a super complex model that makes mine look simplistic … being my intention, as I want to 'Keep It Simple' remember!

Do I need a spreadsheet?

The simple answer is no. You can get started trading or investing in shares without a spreadsheet. If you open an ISA account, then all your dividend income and capital gains from selling shares or funds are tax-free, so there's no need to report anything to the Inland Revenue, nothing to fill in on your Self Assessment tax return.

With your ISA account, you'll know what profit you've made when you sell all your investments and see the total cash, compared to the cash you invested, that's your 'realized' gains … or you can just look at the current value of your portfolio and see your 'prospective' gains.

Investing outside an ISA

If you invest outside an ISA in a general investment account, then you will need to keep track of your dividend income and capital gains during the tax year. You could do this by printing out all your orders – purchase and sales, then match them up, and you could summarise them onto a sheet of paper – but seriously, a spreadsheet is a lot simpler!

The Office for Tax Simplification recommended that the new Capital Gains Tax personal allowances be reduced from £12,300 to between £2,000 and £4,000. Despite these recommendations, the Government confirmed in the March 2021 Budget that the personal allowance for Capital Gains Tax would be frozen until 2026 … so try making the most of it!

I use my ISA allowance and general investment accounts – and I've used three platforms this year, the FreeTrade app, Barclays Smart Investor, and Hargreaves Lansdown – so I feel that I need a spreadsheet to keep track! I also like to monitor my monthly and quarterly performance ... to pat myself on the back or kick myself to try harder!

Calculating share price movements

I use a spreadsheet template to save me repeatedly using my phone's calculator and also to reduce the risk of me getting it wrong – big fat fingers and all that!

It's a good idea to shade 'input' cells to know where you input numbers in the future. Anything without shading is then a calculated field that you don't need to touch again. I've removed the shading to make the pictures clearer to see.

If you copy the following into a spreadsheet, you can check you get the same results. Enter 190 in cell B1 and enter 184 in cell B3. You should enter a formula to calculate the difference in cell B5, so that would be =B1-B3 in this example. Then calculate the percentage increase in cell C5 by entering the formula =B5/B3 which is saying take the difference, and divide it by the lower number to get the percentage difference from 184p to 190p.

	A	B	C
1	Resistance level (ceiling)	190	
2			
3	Support level (floor)	184	
4			
5	Difference	6	0.0326
6			

The decimal 0.0326 is fine, if you want to think that 1 is 100%, 0.1 is 10%, etc. – but I prefer to convert it into a percentage with one decimal place. You do this by clicking to highlight cell C5, then clicking the % icon and the decimal places icon – as shown with arrows below.

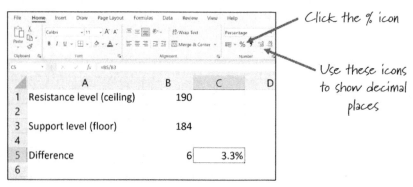

This little template is useful for checking the percentage movements on share prices, to help identify stocks with those +3% movements for share trading.

Estimating costs of a trade

I like to estimate my purchases and keep track of my trading, so the first step is creating the buy cost line. The template I have set up looks like this:

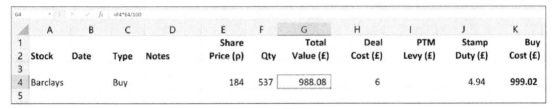

	A	B	C	D	E	F	G	H	I	J	K
G4				=F4*E4/100							
1					Share		Total	Deal	PTM	Stamp	Buy
2	Stock	Date	Type	Notes	Price (p)	Qty	Value (£)	Cost (£)	Levy (£)	Duty (£)	Cost (£)
3											
4	Barclays		Buy		184	537	988.08	6		4.94	999.02
5											

I would normally shade cells E4 and F4, so they are clearly input cells, to enter the purchase price in pence and the quantity.

The formula in cell G4 should be =F4*E4/100 as this converts the total purchase from pence, into pounds and pence.

Enter the transaction purchase cost in cell H4, depending on who you are using, and enter 1 for the PTM levy in cell I4 if the total value was over £10,000.

Also, watch out when calculating the Stamp duty at 0.5%, as this is half of one percent. Remember, if 10% is 0.10, then 1% is 0.01, and half of one percent will be 0.005 so cell J4 will have the formula =G4*0.005

The total purchase costs in cell K4 are calculated by entering =sum(G4:J4)

Estimating profits on your trades

My spreadsheet template shows my trades as two lines, a buy line and a sell line. This is my preferred presentation, given a small laptop screen and worsening eyesight, but you could just as easily continue across to the right and have it all on one line.

	A	B	C	D	E	F	G	H	I	J	K	L	M	N
E5				=E4*1.03										
1					Share		Total	Deal	PTM	Stamp	Buy	Sell	Gain	
2	Stock	Date	Type	Notes	Price (p)	Qty	Value (£)	Cost (£)	Levy (£)	Duty (£)	Cost (£)	Proceeds (£)	£	%
3														
4	Barclays		Buy		184	537	988.08	6		4.94	999.02			
5			Sell	Target +3%	189.52	537	1,017.72	6				1,011.72	13	1.3%
6					5.52									
7														

To start with, I use a formula to calculate a target selling price 3% higher than the buy price. The formula in cell E5 to calculate this is =E4*1.03

The quantity can be made to match that above, so in cell F5, enter =F4

Copy the formula from cell G4 into cell G5. (Click onto cell G4, Ctrl C to copy. Click onto cell G5, Ctrl V to paste).

I've recently added the difference in pence between the buy and sell price in cell E6 as it helps focus my mind, so in cell E6, enter the formula =E5-E4

Enter your dealing costs to sell, then in cell L5, enter the formula =G5-H5-I5 to show the cash received after transaction costs.

The gain in cell M5 is calculated as =L5-K4

The percentage gain is calculated as =M5/K4 then use the % icon and decimal place icon to format the cell to show one decimal place.

Listing out your trades

I use this spreadsheet template to double-check my costs, target my selling price, and also keep track of my trades for tax purposes. I use different spreadsheet tabs – one for
'Holdings' and another for 'Profit Tracker'. So once sold, I cut the lines out of my holdings sheet and add them to my profit tracker sheet.

And that's all I use spreadsheets for - nice and simple!

PART THREE:

Investing in Funds

On reflection:

"The tree is there to climb, but if you fall and break your leg
- don't come running to me"

CHAPTER 13

Getting Started with Funds

Once you get started looking at funds, you can get yourself into a state of paralysis – there are so many options. I've previously spent hours that have turned into days comparing different funds. This is where you need to embrace KIS – Keeping It Simple – by being ruthless on shortlisting, you narrow down your options pretty quickly. In the end, it's well worth it - so I'll share some of my learnings and observations. Let's get started building the foundations!

What is a fund?

A fund is a pool of money from many investors, which the fund managers use to invest in a wide range of investments. Each fund may have a particular focus – growth, income, small-cap, emerging markets, etc.

As an investor, you receive units in the fund. Units represent a portion of the fund's holdings, just like shares represent the portion of holdings in a company.

Why invest in funds?

I now think investing in funds is more effortless than investing in shares. Funds offer a ready-made portfolio of investments that are set up and run by professionals. You can typically invest from £25 to £50. Each fund will explain its minimum investment.

With some platforms, like Hargreaves Lansdown, not charging transaction fees on funds, you could invest your spare cash weekly or monthly, buying what you can afford to set aside. Unlike share trading or share investing, buying funds does not incur the 0.5% stamp duty either, so all your cash is purchasing a piece of the fund.

An example fund

To help me explain, I've selected one of the funds in my portfolio and summarized some of the information provided from my Barclays Smart Investor on 16th April:

Name of the fund – LF Lindsell Train UK Equity, Accumulation

Price – 488.60p (Last price 15/4/21)

Ongoing Charges Figure – 0.65%

Cumulative performance – 1 year, 18.7%

Top 10 holdings – London Stock Exchange (10%), Diageo (9.7%), Relx (9.5%), Schroders (9.2%), Burberry (8.5%), Unilever (8.0%), Mondelez (6.8%), Hargreaves Lansdown (6.6%), Heineken (5.9%), Sage (5.4%). Correct as at 28/2/21.

Countries – UK 79.6%, US 9.7%, Europe 8.7%

Risk Score – 5 (where 1 is lower risk, 7 is a higher risk)

Minimum investments – One-off £50, Regular £50

And some extracts from the Key Investor Information Document:

Fund Objective – To achieve growth in capital and income and provide a total return in excess of the FTSE All-Share Total Return Index after all costs and charges have been taken over at least five years.

Investment Policy – To invest at least 80% of the fund in shares of United Kingdom companies. The fund may invest up to 20% in non-UK companies, cash, and money market instruments. The fund will be concentrated and is unlikely to have more than 35 investments.

Charges for this fund – No entry charge, exit charge, or performance fee. Ongoing charges 0.65%

These are just some of the key features that I pulled out. There's always loads more information to read, past performance charts, etc. So it time to open a bottle of wine and start explaining!

How are funds priced?

This is where most funds are pretty different from shares, as you see a unit price from the day before – not the price right now, today. Each fund will have a valuation point, say at 10 am or mid-day when the fund is priced on the value of the underlying holdings. Fund prices are then updated overnight. The valuation point will be disclosed in the fund information.

This feels a little odd compared to share dealing, as when you buy or sell a fund, it will only be traded after the next valuation point, so depending on your timings, it could take a day or two to find out the exact price that you bought or sold.

Income versus Accumulation

Most funds offer investors the choice between an Income version of the fund, or an Accumulation version, often shortened to Acc.

- **Income** – any income received from dividends from companies in the fund is paid into your trading, ISA, or SIPP account. You can then decide what to do with that income – reinvest it or withdraw and spend it!

- **Accumulation** – this is my preferred choice. Any dividend income is held within the fund and used to purchase more investments, increasing the fund's value compared to its Income equivalent.

The unit prices of the two funds can be quite different, as the accumulation fund benefits from compounding – the income it generates is reinvested to make more money.

When I get older, I will probably move some of my funds into the Income version to create a cash flow without selling any units. But that's still a long way off!

Active versus passive

As you shortlist and review funds, you will see that funds fall into two camps:

- **Actively managed funds:**

  The objective is to exceed their target benchmark. This is my preferred choice!

  There is a professional team monitoring the investments and making changes to the investments in an attempt to maximize the fund's return.

  Active management can move investments from poor performing sectors, or companies, to those offering higher returns. This won't always work out – no one can get it right all of the time, but at least they'll be trying!

- **Passive or 'tracker' funds:**

  Once set up, there is minimal time spent on the fund – this keeps costs a lot lower than managed funds.

  The objective of these funds is to replicate the movements of the market that they're tracking.

  My problem with index tracker funds is that returns are entirely based on the index's performance being tracked – if the market falls, so does the fund.

Past performance

The first thing I look at is the fund's past performance. What percentage return has it achieved in the last few months, last year, three years, five years? I also like to see a graph where the fund performance is hopefully shown exceeding the relevant benchmark index, as that is what I'm expecting from an actively managed fund.

There are always warnings with investments and past performance data. You will keep reading that past performance is no guarantee of future performance, the value of your investment may fall as well as rise, and you might not get back what you put in, etc., etc. – totally agree, but with so many funds to choose from, reducing my selection to only those funds with stronger track records at least narrows my search!

There's frequently a year shown where the growth was low or negative; that's the economic cycle for you – I tend to dismiss any funds with more than one year of low or negative performance.

Another reason why past performance isn't necessarily a reliable indicator of future performance is those fund managers, and their teams change. People naturally move jobs! But at least it's a starting point!

Risk score

The Barclays Smart Investor explains:

"The risk score of a fund – as used in its Key Investor Information Document (KIID) – reflects the significance of the fund's share price fluctuations, usually over five years. Historical performance is not a reliable indicator of the future. A fund's score may change over time. A fund in the lowest category of risk doesn't mean it's risk-free. Generally, the higher the risk category, the more price movement experienced by the fund, and the greater potential for higher returns but also the higher the risk of losing money."

We're all different. At different stages of life we will be looking for something different. At the age of 48, I'm seeking the higher return, accepting the higher risk – so I'm comfortable at a risk score of 5, but I can see that lowering over the coming decades!

Fees

There are typically two categories of costs to consider when investing and holding funds:

Platform and trading fees – for example, from the two platforms that I use:

Hargreaves Lansdown charges 0.45% on the value of funds up to £250k, then 0.25% above that level. They don't charge for the actual buying or selling of funds.

Barclays charge 0.20% on the value of funds and £3 per trade to buy or sell funds.

Fund fees – this is where it gets a little complicated. The same fund provided by different platforms can charge different fees. HL seems to negotiate a lot of discounted fees, so look cheaper than what I've seen elsewhere.

Actively managed funds typically charge ongoing fees over 0.6%, while passive tracker funds only charge around 0.1%

While fund fees are disclosed to you, you don't get to see it as a cost, as they are deducted from within the fund (either from income or selling units of investment).

When in doubt, stop and read – I'd been mistaken into thinking Barclays funds were very costly, as just skimming through it looked like they had more charges than HL. For example, Barclays presents their fund charges as:

- Ongoing charges figure (OCF) 0.65%

- Annual management charge (AMC) 0.60%

So just skimming past, I initially thought you got charged both until I read the explanations and checked the Key Investor Information Document – and realized that the OCF was the total charge, including the annual management charges! As each platform may present costs and other information in different ways, take the time to understand what it is you are reading!

There are loads of providers out there. Lots of them will be cheaper than the two providers that I'm using. You could easily get bogged down reviewing all the different providers, looking at their fund offering and fee structures. Do your research, select a provider and if you are not happy with the fund performance and service after a year, simply move to another provider!

Taxation

Like shares, when funds are held in tax-free ISAs or SIPPs, there's no need to worry about income tax, capital gains tax, or dividend tax.

However, I was surprised to learn from my Barclays Smart Investor that if you use a general investment account to invest in funds, any dividend income reinvested by the fund in an accumulation fund is known as a 'notional distribution' and is taxable – I thought it was just building a larger capital gain for future disposal, not so simple!

Any dividends that are automatically reinvested need to be included in your calculation of dividend income for self-assessment. If your total dividends go over the tax-free allowance of £2,000 (2021/22), then you may have further tax to pay.

To quote from my Barclays Smart Investor:

"When you come to sell accumulation units, you'll pay capital gains tax (CGT) on any increase in value that exceeds your annual CGT allowance – £12,300 for 2021-22. CGT will be payable on the value of the accumulation units when they're sold, minus the original investment and any income that has been accumulated. This means holders of accumulation units should keep a record of all the notional distributions described above, so they can adjust the calculation when they sell their holding, to work out the proportion of their sale proceeds that represents a capital gain."

The income funds may pay out monthly, quarterly or half-yearly. The details are in the Key Information and typically state they are paid out as interest – so that's different from dividend income and has its own annual allowance – who said tax doesn't have to be taxing!

HL pays out the discounts they've negotiated on the funds as 'loyalty bonuses' and politely points out:

"Please note, loyalty bonuses paid outside the ISA and SIPP might be subject to tax. Your Fund and Share Account loyalty bonus gross income is a 'taxable annual payment' to be entered at box 17 of the SA100 tax return, and any tax on this withheld by HL at box 19."

And to finish off taxation, also from Barclays:

"Please bear in mind that tax rules can change in future and their effects on you will depend on your circumstances. Also, remember that whether you buy accumulation or distribution units, they, and any income from them, can fall in value, and you may get back less than you invest."

I love reading those warnings; it's got to be my most read phrase of 2020!

Comparing funds from different platforms

This is where my brain starts to unravel, I'm only using Barclays and Hargreaves Lansdown (HL), and even then, it's still tough to make 'like for like' comparisons, for example, two more funds selected from my portfolio

Baillie Gifford American, Class B, Accumulation.

Barclays and HL both show this fund with the same name, same price, and same past performance, both show ongoing charges as 0.51%, but then HL has negotiated a 0.2% saving, so their net ongoing charge is 0.31%

JPMorgan Emerging Markets, Class B, Accumulation.

Barclays show this fund as JPM Emerging Markets – so it didn't look like Barclays offered this fund on their platform, but a few tweaks to the filters, and I found it. Both have the same price and past performance. Barclays has an ongoing charge of 1.09%, but HL show their ongoing charge as 1.15%, with an HL saving of 0.5%, so an HL net ongoing charge of 0.65%

Comparing the 9 funds that I have, or had, between the two platforms shows that HL have managed to negotiate lower ongoing charges by 0.20%, 0.10%, 0.44%, 0.15%, 0.15%, 0%, 0.22%, 0.15%, and 0.04%. The actual impact of this depends on the value held in each fund. For ease of comparison, I'm simply assuming HL achieves an average saving of 0.15% - the reality is higher or lower!

HL charges a platform fee of 0.45% per annum on the first £250,000 of funds within each HL account and 0.25% per annum on the value of funds between £250,000 and £1m. HL does not charge a fund transaction fee, so there is no cost to buy and sell funds.

Barclays only charge a platform fee of 0.2%, with a minimum of £4 per month. They also charge £3 per transaction to buy or sell funds online.

There's also a tax charge to factor into the comparison, as the HL discount is paid out as a loyalty bonus that is taxable as 'Other Income' if the funds are held outside an ISA or a SIPP, so they deduct 20%. Higher rate taxpayers will then have to pay further tax on this income. Let's assume these funds are within the tax-free wrappers of ISAs or SIPPs!

I've used a spreadsheet to make a 'fag packet' comparison between holdings of £20k, £100k, £250k, and £350k. I've assumed a holding of £20k holds two investments (say £10k each), that the £100k and £250k holds five investments (say £20k and £50k respectively), and that the £350k holds seven investments (say £50k each). I've also assumed these funds are bought and sold within the same year.

This comparison between the Barclays and HL platform charges, transaction fees, and the 0.15% difference on fund charges looks something like this:

On a £20k investment, both cost the same across the year,

On a £100k investment, Barclays is cheaper by £70 across the year,

On a £250k investment, Barclays is cheaper by £220 across the year,

On a £350k investment, Barclays is cheaper by £108 across the year.

From around the £450k level, HL becomes the cheaper option.

The reality is that it depends upon what funds you invest in and how often you buy or sell the funds. Ideally, funds should be purchased and left for a year or two, or even longer, then do a review and make changes as you feel are necessary.

As you build up the value of your funds, it might be possible to transfer your holdings to another provider, 'AS IS', without having to sell and rebuy them - both providers would need to offer the same funds for this to work.

There are loads of alternative platforms, so check out their fees and the costs of their funds!

!!!Warnings!!!

Past performance is not a guide to future returns – but I use them to create a shortlist.

The value of investments will fluctuate and are not guaranteed. This means investors may get back less than they invested – but I think actively managed funds, held for the longer term, must be a lower risk than investing in shares – as professionals are actively managing them!

Invest time in your research - the range of funds you can invest in is vast. Please make sure that you understand the features and risks of any fund before you invest.

Nothing in this book should be construed as personal advice; if you doubt the suitability of an investment for your circumstances, you should seek expert advice.

CHAPTER 14

Barclays Funds

While Barclays is both my bank and my share dealing platform, I find their research website dated and a touch annoying. You need to be logged into your online banking, and I frequently get timed out. The material is excellent, but I don't find the site as easy to use as the HL site – that said, let's walk through how Barclays present their funds offering.

Barclays Smart Investor

When I checked today, 16th April 2021, there were 2,470 funds, 987 Exchange Traded Funds, 326 Investment Trusts, and 121 Gilts & Bonds – in addition to the 1,413 shares - on Smart Investor!

Once you click into a particular fund, there are a few tabs of summary information provided by Barclays. You need to open the Factsheet attachment and the KIID attachment – these give far more information and are more interesting to read, covering fund objectives and policy, portfolio manager comments, risk and reward profiles, charges, and past performance. If you're going to invest, you need to get into your research and start reading all this stuff – preparation pays!

With so many to look at, it's easier to use the shortlists already created by Barclays. I've done that before, and it's worth a try – but I now prefer to use the HL website to search, read and select my funds – it's just more user-friendly!

The Barclays Funds List

This is one way of reducing the 2,470 funds down to just 65. Barclays' investment specialists selected the list of funds they believe have built solid reputations, can demonstrate robust investment processes, and have the potential to generate consistent returns in the medium to long term – being five years or more.

The team follows three main steps when deciding whether or not a fund should be included on the list. This is an extract from their explanation:

"Step 1: Assessing risk and return

One of the key criteria that we assess is the relationship between risk and return. This means we compare the amount of risk the fund manager has taken to achieve the expected returns. We want to make sure fund managers aren't taking too many risks in trying to get you good returns on your investment. We also analyze how consistent the fund manager's approach and past returns have been and the level of experience of the rest of the fund's investment team.

Step 2: Our due diligence

Once we feel that a fund meets our high standards, we start the next stage, which involves extensive manager due diligence. Our process can be divided into two distinct steps: investment due diligence and operational due diligence.

Investment due diligence looks for the best-in-class managers. We use our '5P' research framework to assess and score the manager in five key areas: Parent, People, Philosophy, Process, and Performance. A good score in each of these five areas is critical to the likelihood of future success.

Operational due diligence aims to assess and mitigate business and operational risks. This means we will look at whether the fund manager has the business resources and processes needed to support the investment activities and the operational know-how required to deliver and sustain the investment strategy.

Step 3: Selection approval process

Our team of investment professionals then comes to a joint decision about whether the fund deserves to be included on our list. This helps us make sure our decisions are consistent and free from individual bias.

Once a fund has been selected through our investment research, we then make sure we can offer you the best share class we can, so that as little as possible of your investment is eaten up in fund charges."

So, it's a great place to start reviewing funds that have been shortlisted – but that doesn't mean I would invest in all of them. It's a list that will appeal to a broad audience, with different risk appetites and different requirements – so, as I said, it's only the start – you now need to put the time and effort into reviewing and shortlisting those that appeal to you!

Ready-made investments

Another alternative, making it even more straightforward – is their five ready-made investments with different characteristics and risk profiles. They mix cash, bonds, and shares. Cash is the least risky, shares are the riskiest, and bonds sit somewhere in between. These five are shown as:

- "**Defensive** – *our lowest risk fund, but there's no such thing as risk-free.*

- **Cautious** – *slightly higher risk than Defensive, but still at the lower end of the spectrum.*

- **Balanced** – *medium risk. Some uncertainty, but within your comfort zone.*

- **Growth** – *higher risk, designed for those who'll take chances if the potential payouts are worth it.*

- **Adventurous** – *our highest risk fund, it's for those who can afford to take the biggest risk of loss for the chance of getting the biggest reward."*

I've not touched these, as I prefer to create my own mix of investments - but they might be worth a look for you ... have a read!

CHAPTER **15**

Hargreaves Lansdown Funds

I find the Hargreaves Lansdown (HL) website particularly easy to navigate and is excellent for researching funds ... of which they had 3,672 on my last check! It's just an easy site to explore and shortlist funds – here's how to do it:

Wealth Shortlist

An excellent place to start with the HL funds is with their 'Wealth Shortlist', which reduced the number down to 121 funds. This 'shortlist' helps identify funds with the most significant performance potential, based on the following HL assessments:

- "**Manager** - *The individual or team behind a fund is its driving force. We look for experienced managers with plenty of research resources and support.*

- **Process** - *A manager's stock selection and style determine what they buy and when. We like managers who consistently apply their strict processes through different market conditions.*

- **Culture** - *We dig behind the scenes to evaluate how fund managers and their teams operate. We'll also look at their approach to Environmental, Social, and Governance factors and management companies' purpose, reward structure, and leadership.*

- **Performance** - *We look at each manager's performance after charges to find managers who are truly adding value for investors. We want at least five years of applicable data, ideally ten."*

The filters are straightforward to use, which helps you narrow them down further. I walk through what I did later.

Shortlists

The menu also offers some pre-built filter criteria, which shortlists:

- Funds for income

- Seeking retirement income

- Established trackers

Popular Funds

This is nice; it simply provides a list of the most popular ten funds – so an easy bit of research to open and read each one, most you'll dismiss, but it might identify one or two you like.

Master Portfolios

These are designed to help you start investing, providing five example portfolios depending on your aims and attitude to risk. The underlying funds are selected from the Wealth Shortlist, which you can tailor by changing the percentage invested in each fund according to your preferences.

- "**Adventurous** - *This portfolio aims to generate a high level of growth and invests in higher-risk areas like emerging markets and smaller companies.*

- **Medium risk** - *This medium-risk portfolio aims for a reasonable return with less volatility than more aggressive options.*

- **Conservative** - *This defensive portfolio aims for modest growth with relatively low volatility, though it can still fall in value.*

- **Investing for children** - *Children usually have a long investment horizon, so this portfolio invests in higher-risk areas with greater growth potential.*

- **Investing for income** - *This income portfolio is designed to produce a good level of income with the potential to grow and keep pace with inflation."*

If you select one of these and insert an investment value, it provides the list of funds and a proposed percentage holding of each that you can amend to suit your tastes.

I checked out the 'Adventurous' one, which comprised seven funds, including the Legal & General US Index, the Threadneedle European Select and the JPM Emerging Markets that I'm holding – so I guess that badges me as an adventurous Dad !!!

CHAPTER 16

Index Trackers

Trackers are called 'passive' investments and are typically a cheaper way of tracking market indices and specific sectors' performance compared to actively managed funds.

Trackers can either be Exchange Traded Funds (ETFs), unit trusts, or Open-Ended Investment Companies (OEICs).

I invested in my first tracker back in 2018. I sold it earlier this year – as I've decided to focus on actively managed funds attempting to deliver higher returns than their target benchmark index.

Everyone is different, so it's still worth covering index trackers – and it answers one of my pre-pandemic questions, how do you buy into gold … as my wife's eyes light up, more jewelry? Sorry dear, I was thinking about an ETF!

Exchange-Traded Funds (ETF's)

An ETF trades on the stock exchange. You can buy and sell an ETF like shares in a company. This means you have the comfort of knowing at what price you are buying or selling.

The first ETF was listed on the London Stock Exchange's Main Market in April 2000. After the abolition of stamp duty on ETFs in February 2007, the London Stock Exchange became the leading European center for ETFs, with more than 1,200 ETFs listed on its Main Market.

There are two main types of ETF – physical and synthetic:

- **Physical ETF** - invests directly in whatever stocks it is tracking.

  For example, a FTSE 100 tracker invests in the shares of companies that make up the FTSE 100 Index, while a gold ETF invests in gold bullion held in a vault. When you invest in an ETF, you buy a stake in the ETF, not the index being tracked or the underlying investment.

- **Synthetic ETF** - uses derivatives to gain exposure to a particular market.

  Synthetic ETFs are more complex and are riskier than physical ETFs due to what's known as 'counterparty risk', which means if the investment bank that has sold the derivative can't meet its obligations, you could lose out.

Physical ETFs are easier to understand and are less vulnerable to hidden risks, so they're more suitable for individual investors. That said, your money is still at risk. As with other types of investment, the value can fall, meaning you end up with less than you invest.

Open-Ended Investment Companies (OEICs) and unit trusts

This is a legal structure used for funds. Both are' open-ended', which means the fund manager creates new shares in the OEIC and new units in unit trusts when you buy and cancels them when you sell.

The value of these shares and units directly reflects the value of the underlying investments held in the fund and is not known when you place your order to buy or sell – prices are determined at the next valuation point.

This type of legal structure is used for both passive funds and actively managed funds. The fund will clearly say what they are.

Fees

Barclays charge ETF's like shares, so a 0.1% annual customer fee and £6 online transaction fee.

OEICs and unit trusts are classed as funds, so Barclays charge a 0.2% annual customer fee and a £3 online transaction fee.

As trackers, the ongoing charges deducted by the investment provider should be low, a lot lower than actively managed funds – but these need to be compared as well.

Pricing

ETFs are like shares, so supply and demand dynamics will impact the price at which they trade.

The price of OEICs and unit trusts are calculated on the value of the underlying investments.

!!!Warning!!!

Risk is unavoidable when you invest. If the value of your investment falls, you could end up getting back less than you originally put in. But there's increased risk when you invest in an ETF – specifically a synthetic ETF.

CHAPTER 17

My Funds Experience So Far

This chapter steps through what I do and why I do it. I believe it's easy to get paralyzed with loads of options and information overload, so the approach I adopt for everything in life is to break the task down into bite-size chunks, keep a view of the bigger picture, and crack on – monitor, review, amend as necessary – but move forward! Keep It Simple!

I don't view myself as a risk-taker – I don't do hand gliding or parachuting, rock climbing, or caving – but friends and family seem to think otherwise and can refer to different examples of my career choices, house purchases, renovation, and extension projects – so maybe I do embrace risk, but I always ensure it's a mitigated risk – that is, I have a backup plan or an exit plan.

My view on selecting funds will be unique to me; everyone is different – you must do what is right for you. What I want this chapter to do, is to help you see how easy it is to get into funds.

I want my family to invest in funds from a young age. My guidance to them is to hold some cash but invest in funds. Skip the share trading and the investing in individual company shares – skip straight to funds!

How I got into funds

I had never used funds. It's one of my biggest mistakes! All those years, I'd held cash in savings accounts, Premium Bonds, under the mattress, and in the wife's wallet – never a great idea!

Things changed for me when I decided to take control of my pension. Over the years, bouncing from one company to the next, I had around nine small pensions spread around. I paid little attention to where they were invested or what the fees were. I just knew they weren't going to provide much of a retirement.

By my 40th, I wondered whether I would ever get to retire. I'd quit a job on the birth of our first child to set up on my own, going freelance – that started years of interim projects working as a consultant or being employed for the project, initially near home in the Midlands, to then further away up in Cheshire and down as far as Norwich, then came the international roles – flying out to the US once a month, and in between times visiting the businesses in France, Italy and Spain. It sounds like fun, but it takes its toll – eat, sleep and repeat – not something I wanted to keep doing, not when I had three kids growing up fast!

I finally researched SIPPs, Self Invested Pension Plans and opened one with Hargreaves Lansdown (HL). I then went through the admin of transferring each of my pensions into the SIPP and was quite pleased with the total – although still far off a decent retirement.

Once in the SIPP, I started research on funds to invest in – I found the HL website and investor support materials handy and spread my investment across several funds.

Pensions are long-term investments, so you can sit back and let them grow. But it's still wise to monitor your investments and make changes as and when it's necessary.

Taking charge of my pension

I made my first fund purchases in my SIPP in August 2018. Despite the Covid-19 pandemic, the funds performed well – when I did my most recent review at the start of March 2021 – two and a half years in, the four funds were showing the following gains:

- ASI UK Smaller Companies – 38% gain

- Legal & General US Index – 31% gain

- Lindsell Train Global Equity – 20% gain

- Baillie Gifford Global Discovery – 89% gain!

If I'd have had an equal weighting in each fund, the weighted average was a 45% gain … for two and a half years, and through the pandemic … I was happy with that! That's an average of 16% growth each year!

Compounding effect

Compounding plays an essential part in building gains, as you make gains on your previous gains. Let's take a three-year example, if you invested £1,000 and achieved a 10% growth each year:

- By the end of year 1, the £1,000 is now worth £1,100

- By the end of year 2, the £1,100 is now worth £1,210

- By the end of year 3, the £1,210 is now worth £1,331

Over the three years, the cumulative (total) gain is £331 on the £1,000 invested, so that's 33.1% across the three years.

So the smart choice, if possible, is to reinvest income from investments or choose accumulation funds that reinvest automatically!

Investing in Funds

I think the most challenging part with funds is selecting them - once that's done, funds make for an easy monthly investment, or as and when you have some surplus cash to invest.

I like to hold a variety of funds, which I think spreads my risk. I'm holding funds covering the UK, Europe, US, and Emerging Markets. I'm also holding more than one fund in each category, as the top 10 investments show different company names.

I feel more comfortable investing in funds than investing in shares, as I'm buying a ready-made portfolio that is being actively managed. I feel a blind spot with shares if I'm not monitoring the share price and company performance.

I'm also more comfortable viewing funds as a longer-term investment, whereas with shares, I tend to sell when my gains are looking good!

I concluded it was also time to get my kids into funds – we've been lazy parents leaving Christmas, Birthday, and pocket money in low-interest bank accounts, as that's how I was brought up – it was time to move the kids into investing in funds – tax-free, courtesy of Junior Stocks & Shares ISA's.

With Junior ISA's, the child takes ownership at age 18, and then it's their choice. Until then, the money can't be touched – so we've agreed to keep some cash for spending, some for investing, and if they want the invested cash before they turn 18 (i.e., the eldest son is saving for his first car at age 17) – then the bank of mum & dad will loan them the money ... for repayment when they get access to their ISA at age 18.

I spent some time shortlisting funds at the start of March, and we had a family Saturday discussing finance and reviewing the two-page summaries I'd prepared on each fund – my wife's eyes glazed over, my darling 13-year-old daughter was like, that's ages away, the roll of eyes, etc., etc. But there was hope; my 15-year-old son got it, he's studying GCSE Business Studies, and his car purchase ambitions shot through the roof!

How I shortlisted some funds

Lesson from the past, the Hargreaves Lansdown site is so easy to use, filter, and read – so that's where I started – with their search funds filter. Without filters, it was showing 3,656 funds – so I applied the following filters:

Sector – of the 40 or so options, I selected: Europe excluding UK, Europe including UK, European smaller companies, Global emerging markets, North America, North American smaller cos, Specialist, Targeted absolute return, Technology & Telecoms, UK all companies, UK equity income & growth, UK smaller companies, Unclassified and Volatility managed ... they sounded good, even if some of their names made no sense at the time! I skipped about half the sectors, as I didn't want mixed investments, bonds, property, or specific China or Japan funds.

Unit type – this is either 'Income' or 'Accumulation'. I prefer the accumulation. I did have an Income fund in my SIPP but had ticked the HL box to reinvest any income back into the fund, so the units held kept increasing – and HL doesn't charge for dealing in funds – but why go through that whole cycle!

Fund type – this is either 'Actively Managed' or 'Tracker'. I prefer to pay the higher fees and have an actively managed fund, as they are actively trying to beat their target benchmark index.

Wealth Shortlist – tick box, yes – might as well narrow down the funds HL has already shortlisted!

After those criteria were applied, the staggering 3,656 funds were reduced down to just 19 funds – now that is easier to review!

How and why I shortlisted further

So 19 funds was an excellent place to start, but I wasn't going to discuss 19 options with the family – so I printed the list of 19 funds and clicked into each one, just picking out some of the key features that I was particularly interested in – fund size, number of companies invested in, ongoing charges, 5-year annual performance - and I noted those on the list. I dismissed funds for the following reasons:

- **Small funds**, with holdings in the millions rather than billions. So £80m was struck off, but £1,914 million stayed on! This could have been an oversight on my part, but I figured funds with higher holdings must be more popular.

- **Funds invested in a small portfolio of companies,** so one investing in just 25 companies was binned – again, maybe that was a wrong decision, but I wanted funds with a more extensive portfolio of investments as this reduces risk – I still recall 60 as being the magic number for an effective portfolio effect from my studies years ago!

- **Ongoing charges** – while I'm willing to pay more for a managed fund, I'm only happy with charges in the 0.3% to 0.9% range - so a fund at 1.11% got binned. There's no time for getting paralyzed. You need to make a decision and move on – right or wrong!

- **5-year performance** – so while all the warnings say past returns may not continue into the future … I still take the view that it's a good indication of how the fund might perform in the future. A fund was dismissed for only having a 2-year track record, and another was dismissed for having losses in three of the five years. I still needed to reduce the list further, so I knocked out funds with losses in 2 of the five years and funds with low returns in 2 or more years.

The ten funds I offered my kids

The efforts of shortlisting the HL Wealth list brought it down to just four funds, but I added one of my dismissed funds into the mix to see if the kids would like ... a Unicorn fund!

The first five funds were shortlisted from the HL Wealth list, the following four were from my 2018 SIPP selection, and the last one I'd recently added to my SIPP – so the ten funds I discussed with the kids were:

- Baillie Gifford American (Class B) Accumulation

- JPM Emerging Markets (Class B) Accumulation

- Marlborough UK Micro-Cap Growth (Class P) Accumulation

- Threadneedle European Select (Class Z) Accumulation

- Unicorn Outstanding British Companies (Class B) Accumulation

- ASI UK Smaller Companies (Class S) Accumulation

- Legal & General US Index (Class C) Accumulation

- Lindsell Train Global Equity (Class D) Income

- Baillie Gifford Global Discovery (Class B) Accumulation

- LF Lindsell Train UK Equity (Class D) Accumulation

I was pretty happy with this, as it covered the UK, the US, Europe, and Emerging Markets – so selecting just one fund from each area could quickly generate an excellent portfolio spread across the globe!

Having now seen the HL Master Portfolio – 'Adventurous' – I'm going to adopt two of the funds from that list, so the kids will also get offered:

- Rathbone Global Opportunities (Class S) Accumulation

- Jupiter Global Value Equity (Class X) Accumulation

The Jupiter fund doesn't pass my shortlisting approach, but I like the top 10 companies in the fund - including Aviva from my recent dividend investment, B&Q owner Kingfisher, Volkswagen who is doing well with electric cars, and could be a strong challenger to Tesla, and Ralph Lauren.

How has the shortlist performed?

I've compared the fund prices from the pack I presented to the family, prices ranging from 3rd to 5th March, to the latest prices as I'm writing this at 16th April - and updated on 7th May.

The 16th April review looked good - only one fund was down, one was up less than 3%, three were up around 6%, two were up between 7-8%, and three were up about 10%.

The 7th May review reflected another tech sell off in the US, with three of the funds down against the start of March, one fund up nearly 5%, three funds were up between 7-9%, and three funds were up between 10-12%.

Fund	5th March	16th April	7th May
Baillie Gifford American	1,914p	Up 6.1% to 2,030p	Down 7.1% to 1,778p
JPM Emerging Markets	466.6p	Down 1.4% to 460.1p	Down 3.7% to 449.4p
Marlborough UK Micro-Cap Growth	1,059p	Up 10.1% to 1,165.87p	Up 12.3% to 1,189.13
Threadneedle European Select	252.7p	Up 10.0% to 277.86p	Up 10.7% to 279.8p
Unicorn Outstanding British Companies	324p	Up 7.2% to 347.19p	Up 7.4% to 348.1p
ASI UK Smaller Companies	124.2p	Up 8.3% to 134.5p	Up 9.4% to 135.9p
Legal & General US Index	723.1p	Up 10.9% to 801.9p	Up 10.6% to 799.5p
Lindsell Train Global Equity	277.4p	Up 6.3% to 294.86p	Up 4.8% to 290.8p
Baillie Gifford Global Discovery	2,826p	Up 2.8% to 2,905p	Down 8.1% to 2,597p
LF Lindsell Train UK Equity,	189.4p	Up 6.4% to 201.51p	Up 7.9% to 204.5p

Monitoring the performance of my shortlist highlighted the need to spread investments across several funds. It also showed how well the US Index fund had performed compared to the managed American fund - so holding both is now my plan! It also showed that my dismissed fund - the Unicorn fund - outperformed four of my selected funds!

How is the Junior ISA performing?

So my eldest son, the 15-year-old, selected three funds to get started with ... he choose the ASI UK Smaller Companies fund, the Baillie Gifford American fund, and the JPM Emerging Markets fund – investing the same in each.

Ideally, funds should be reviewed perhaps monthly, quarterly or half yearly - they need to be left to grow. That said, we've been monitoring each week - during a lot of US market volatility. The story so far is:

Saturday Review	UK Fund	American Fund	Emerging Markets Fund	Overall Performance
20th March	Up 0.3%	Down 4.1%	Down 2.4%	Down 2.1%
27th March	Up 1.3%	Down 6.4%	Down 3.9%	Down 3.0%
3rd April	Up 2.4%	Down 4.3%	Down 1.2%	Down 1.0%
10th April	Up 6.9%	Up 1.1%	Up 0.2%	Up 2.7%
17th April	Up 8.8%	Up 4.2%	Down 0.4%	Up 4.2%
24th April	Up 9.7%	Down 0.6%	Down 0.5%	Up 2.9%
1st May	Up 10.0%	Up 1.9%	Down 0.4%	Up 3.8%
8th May	Up 10.0%	Down 8.8%	Down 2.7%	Down 0.5%
15th May	Up 8.3%	Down 14.6%	Down 7.2%	Down 4.5%

The weekly chat ...

Week 1 - we've only just started.

Week 2 - the markets are very volatile right now!

Week 3 - stop looking at the bad news, let the funds ride it out!

Week 4 - smile – we're finally up!

Week 5 - phew, overall up 4% - Dad breathes a sigh of relief!

... Week 8 & 9 - with the stock market volatility in the US, we really need to stop looking at these weekly! Keep calm, remain patient, smile!

In the coming months, we'll be adding another UK fund, the Europe fund, and the Jupiter Global Value fund to this Junior ISA, which will help diversify the overall investment.

Child Trust Funds

These tax-free savings accounts for children were launched in 2005 to encourage families to save for their children's future. The scheme was scrapped in 2011, with parents now allowed to move their Child Trust Funds into Junior ISA's.

While our eldest child had missed having a Child Trust Fund, my wife had set them up for our youngest kids when they were born, with a low monthly direct debit - lucky them!

Both Child Trust Fund's were with different providers, they were charging 1.5% commission each year, and we were not monitoring the investment returns. Bad mistake. We should have moved them years ago - oops

Setting up a Junior Stocks & Shares ISA for the eldest was easy. I used HL, applied online, funded the account, and made the investments - done.

I read that you couldn't open a Junior ISA if they already had a Child Trust Fund, but you could transfer an existing Child Trust Fund into a Junior ISA - so that's what we did, and we're still waiting - amazing, eight weeks later!

Looking at the annual charges, it looks like we'll also be saving money. The three funds our son selected charge ongoing fees of 0.31%, 0.65%, and 0.77%. HL charges a platform fee of 0.45% with no transaction costs for funds - so we're effectively now paying 0.76% on one fund, 1.1% on another, and 1.22% on another – all below the 1.5% charged by the Child Trust Funds! I also feel that we'll get a far more significant growth as well!

Tracker funds are even cheaper, so if we have a couple of tracker investments, they'll be running at a third of the Child Trust Fund annual charges!

Closing thoughts...

It's time to wrap this up – we've covered the background to help build a foundation of knowledge and understanding, we've stepped through researching, trading, investing, buying, and selling shares, and we've simplified the world of funds. There's plenty to go at, still with risk – there's always risk, but hopefully a lower risk than cryptocurrency, Contracts For Difference (CFDs), index trading, small-cap companies, etc., etc.

Keep It Simple. If you don't understand it, don't do it.

I've shared my thoughts and experiences, the things I do, and why I do them. I hope you found this guide easy to read, informative, and easy to understand. If nothing else, I hope this guide has inspired you to become an intelligent investor – invest your time and effort in research, build up your knowledge and understanding - start small, and learn some lessons with a lower risk approach to investing.

Don't follow the herd, don't take high-risk gambles, just do your own thing and do it well.

Enjoy, have fun, but proceed with caution - while I've made some good money from trading in shares, from dividends, and the growth of funds – I have also experienced losses. You can't get it right all the time. I hope I've used enough examples to demonstrate how volatile and unpredictable the stock market can be – in the bad times, it defies belief, it can be frustrating and worrying. But, in the good times – it's amazing, rewarding, and well worth the effort ... so I guess investing is very much like parenting!

Good luck, take care, and stay safe!

Patrick Carter

Referrals, Reviews, and Feedback

FreeTrade Referral

If you have a friend using the FreeTrade app, ask them to send you a referral link – that way, both you and your friend will receive a mystery share after you open and fund your account.

If not, I'm happy to share my referral link –please use the address below:

https://magic.freetrade.io/join/paul/ddca152f

Reviews

Please review this book!

I always head to reviews before buying stuff, it can be quite insightful reading the good and not-so-good feedback.

Reviews help authors more than you think. If you enjoyed this book, or even if you didn't, please consider leaving a review online – it would be greatly appreciated

Feedback

I'd love to hear your feedback and suggestions for future content, but one thing I can't do is offer advice as to whether you should buy, sell or hold anything - that's a regulated activity, sorry.

If you find any mistakes in this book, my apologies - please let me know, and I'll get them corrected.

My email address is ppcarter73@outlook.com

Many thanks, best wishes,

Patrick Carter

COMING SOON ...

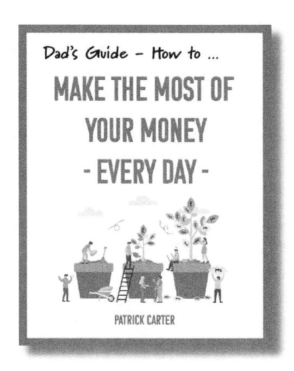

The first challenge for anyone wanting to invest in shares and funds is ... having the spare cash to invest!

This easy-reading guide comes from five decades of knowledge and experience from a finance professional sharing life's learnings and observations.

Applicable to all, from student to family, this guide provides a framework for reviewing, controlling, and improving personal finances.

Most people have waste. It happens. But that waste builds up over time and becomes quite surprising once identified. If you are looking for a place to start but are unsure what, where, or how? Then read this book, follow the steps, use the templates, and make the most of your money, every day!

Full of hints, tips, and money-saving ideas, plus some easy 'side hustles' to earn a little money along the way!

Printed in Great Britain
by Amazon